THE IDEA OF CHRISTIAN CHARITY

LIBRARY OF RELIGIOUS PHILOSOPHY

Thomas V. Morris, editor

Volume 3

THE IDEA OF CHRISTIAN CHARITY

A CRITIQUE OF SOME CONTEMPORARY CONCEPTIONS

GORDON GRAHAM

University of Notre Dame Press
Notre Dame   London

Library of Congress Cataloging-in-Publication Data

Graham, Gordon.
    The idea of Christian charity : a critique of some
contemporary conceptions / Gordon Graham.
        p. cm. – (Library of religious philosophy ; v. 3)
    Includes bibliographical references.
    ISBN 0-268-01167-2
    1. Charity. I. Title. II. Series.
BV4639.G67   1990
241'.4–dc20   89-29257

For my brother

ALASTAIR

priest and social worker

CONTENTS

ACKNOWLEDGMENTS

Among the many people with whom I have discussed the questions in this book I am especially grateful to Prof. David Scott of Virginia Theological Seminary, Dr. Robert K. Fullinwider of the University of Maryland, College Park, and Hugh La-Follette of East Tennessee State University.

A small part of chapter two first appeared in *New Blackfriars*, and parts of chapter three first appeared in *Philosophy* and *Modern Theology*. I am grateful to the editors of these journals for permission to use this material.

I am also very grateful to Mrs. Janet Kirk and Mrs. Anne Cameron for their speedy and efficient preparation of the final typescript and to Mr. Hugh Upton for help in proofreading.

INTRODUCTION

This is an age of professionalism. Where once the professions consisted in law, medicine, and the Church, now everything from advertising to town planning is so regarded, and accordingly each brings with it the trappings of professionalism – self-governing institutions, specialized training, and distinctive qualifications. Something of the same phenomenon is to be found in the world of the academic where 'professionalism' within different disciplines both causes and is fostered by increasingly specialized courses, degrees, books, and journals.

No doubt a high degree of specialization is almost inevitable as human knowledge grows, and, on the grounds that the division of labor increases productivity to the benefit of all, it is by and large to be welcomed. But it also has its costs. Chief among these is the increasing isolation of subjects from each other, even subjects like philosophy and theology which have a large number of common concerns. This isolation has two aspects. First, it prevents cross-fertilization of ideas. This drawback should not be exaggerated, however, because in general the amount of knowledge and expertise which almost all fields of modern learning require makes the scope for really profitable interdisciplinary collaboration very limited. What is more important is the tendency of professional isolation to increase the risk of intellectual in-breeding, that is, the perpetuation of error or misunderstanding in fundamental assumptions and *methods* of inquiry. It increases the danger, in other words, that something which ought to be an academic *discipline* degenerates into a mere school of thought.

Philosophy, though it too has suffered from professionalism, is less prone to this particular corruption, perhaps, because from its beginning it has itself consisted in large part precisely in a critical examination of the foundations of thought and the assumptions upon which theories are erected. So too with theology, which, since Aquinas at least, has regularly drawn upon the findings of a variety of philosophical, historical, and scientific disciplines. It is all the more surprising, therefore, that one of the casualties of professionalism has been philosophical theology. With one or two notable exceptions, philosophers in the Anglo-Saxon and Continental traditions no longer concern themselves with theological questions and theologians, by and large, are unfamiliar with and unsympathetic to modern philosophy. The exceptions are to be found in the area of metaphysics and natural theology. The divorce between moral theology and moral philosophy is almost complete.

Yet, as I hope to show, it is precisely in this area that there are many important and topical subjects where the explorations of a properly philosophical theology are both interesting and fruitful, and where, curiously, the methods of modern philosophy give us reason to return to older and more orthodox lines of thought which modern theology has been inclined to regard as outmoded.

My belief, then, is that there is philosophical theology to be done, but since I am myself a product of a world of academic specialization, it would be foolish to think that I could do much more than make an effort in the right direction. My basic approach remains philosophical, and may, despite my efforts, appear as nothing more than an intrusion by philosophy into theological questions. Such intrusions have rarely been welcomed by the practitioners of other disciplines, whose reaction has generally been similar to that of the various "experts" whom Socrates chooses to examine in Plato's earlier dialogues, namely an indignant rejection of the philosophers' questions in the belief that they are in some way irrelevant and arise out of ignorance or eccentricity.

No doubt this response has been justified on many occasions, for the traditional scope of their subject has tended to breed intellectual arrogance on the part of philosophers. Nevertheless, there have been occasions when philosophers have presented serious intellectual challenges to beliefs and methods whose truth and validity are generally assumed, and in doing so shown that what has commonly passed for intellectual progress is a mere fashion in thought.

Philosophy, of course, is not merely criticism, but at a time of increased academic specialization with its attendant dangers this particular role becomes especially important. Its best model is the Socratic dialectic, which strives to remain as open-minded as possible, raising fundamental criticisms but never presupposing that they cannot be answered. This is, of course, an ideal unlikely to be wholly realized, but this short book attempts to realize something like it. It is offered primarily as a challenge to some fashionable ways of thinking. I have attempted to look as critically, but also as positively and sympathetically as I can at certain strands of thought in Christian ethics and to bring to bear upon them the sorts of consideration and the type of analysis that contemporary philosophy employs.

There is a danger, with such an enterprise, that instead of building a bridge it falls between two stools. Inevitably the argument involves areas of thought and inquiry in which I am inexpert, notably biblical criticism and psychotherapy but also economics and history. I have, so far as possible, relied on the best material in these areas available to the "intelligent layman," and tried to signal the points at which issues arise where I am simply relying on the judgment of others. No doubt there remain some relatively simple errors but I do not know that these create a serious obstacle to the enterprise in which I am engaged. For the aim is not to show that my criticisms are unanswerable, but that they require answers, and to point to directions of thought, themselves fairly orthodox, which have tended to be overlooked and which might supply the answers. More importantly, in an attempt to deflect the charge of inexpert blundering, I have endeavored, again in the spirit of the Socratic dialectic, to provide reasoned arguments in support both of criticisms I make and conclusions I reach, and while I do not suppose for a moment that my judgment or learning is superior to that of the writers I criticize, I do think that the arguments I present are strong enough to show the need for some reply.

At any rate my purpose will have been served if I can prompt some reexamination of the idea of Christian charity.

CHAPTER ONE

KERYGMA AND ETHICS

There are a number of problems that may be raised about the relation between theology and ethics. One is a logical problem, familiar to philosophers since the time of Plato, about how God, or any god, can, as it were, underwrite morality. Can it make the moral law any more or less certain, any more or less binding, if it comes from God? Surely we must and do use our sense of right and wrong to judge whether those commandments which purport to be divine are indeed from God? This, however, is not the problem I want to discuss. It is, it seems to me, one that arises for all monotheistic religions, and if it is more usually associated with Christianity in our minds, this is only because Christian theology has had more to do with philosophy than has the theology of any other religion.

More important, in a sense, than the problem "How does morality come from God?" is the question "How does a distinctively Christian ethic arise from the Christian Gospel of God?" And in its turn this question raises two further questions: "Just what *is* the Christian ethic?" and "Just what is the heart of the Christian Gospel?" It might be supposed, with justice, that these two questions could only be answered at enormous length. So extensive is the history of Christian theology and so wide the disagreements in it, that it really seems quite foolish to ask and try to answer such fundamental questions except in the context of something the size of Aquinas's *Summa*

1

Theologica or Barth's *Church Dogmatics,* and even then, it might reasonably be suggested, no very clear or determinate answer is likely to emerge.

On the other hand, even such great works as these have to be assimilated and assessed by individuals if they are to possess any understanding of their own, and this assessment will be made for the most part by those who are less expert and who, for their own purposes, need a general overview which omits but does not contradict the scholarly detail. There is reason to believe, therefore, that though *everything* concerning Christian theology and ethics cannot be said in a small compass, *something* may be said, which by its very generality and relative brevity is more useful for certain purposes. It is in the light of such belief that I propose to address these two questions as a preliminary to focusing upon the idea of Christian charity.

I

I said that there are two questions to consider, but in fact their separation can only be temporary. It is the thesis of this first chapter that the "ethics" and the "theology" of Christianity cannot be isolated one from the other, that the pattern of thought and conduct Christianity commands is not so much a morality as a religious ethic. It was at one time supposed by what was known as "liberal" Christianity, and what I shall call "ethical Christianity," that Christian morality could indeed be separated from its theology and even regarded as central to Christian teaching. The motivation for this is evident enough. In a world like the Western world since the latter half of the nineteenth century, in which it has become difficult to believe in miraculous happenings such as the Virgin Birth, the miracles, and the Resurrection, but where nonetheless there is a residual desire to preserve traditional religion, it was (and still is often) thought easier to subscribe to the moral beliefs associated with Christianity if we forget the supernatural context in which they are customarily set. Hence it is seen as desirable to promote 'Christianity' as a morality rather than a theology. In this way, the notion of a Christian changes from one who believes certain historical events to have taken place and to have a profound theological significance to one who subscribes to or even just acts out a certain code of conduct. Thus many avowed secularists and even atheists have been, contrary to their own opinions, declared 'true Christians' by those of this "liberal" persuasion.

The change of view briefly alluded to here describes a major event in the history of Christian thought and self-understanding, namely that which took place in the course of the nineteenth century. It is one which Edmund Gosse recorded from first-hand experience in his celebrated book *Father and Son*. Gosse's portrait of his father is of an almost fanatical exemplar of nineteenth-century Protestantism, but as Gosse himself remarks, his father's religion, though extreme, shares with almost all the versions of Christianity that preceded it an overriding concern with the intellectual and doctrinal content of religion to the near total exclusion of questions of conduct, while that which succeeded it, the liberal Christianity, which had come to prominence at the time Gosse was writing (1905), made conduct the center of religion.

No doubt the excessive emphasis on doctrine which marked a great deal of nineteenth-century Christianity was bound, sooner or later, to produce a swing in the opposite direction, partly because religious belief cannot be reduced to subscription to theological doctrine. But the attempt to isolate a Christian code of conduct freed from the theological concerns of the Gospel is equally onesided, and hopeless. A number of considerations taken together show this conclusively. To begin with, there is the question of the source from which any ethic might be distilled. Suppose we focus on the New Testament. It becomes obvious after a little reflection that there are at least three rather different ethical emphases in it. There is first the ethos of Matthew's Gospel, next that of the Johannine literature, and third that of Paul's Epistles.[1] There may, of course, be ways in which these different strands of thought could be unified (though this is not obvious) but their initial differences are sufficient to make the point that the quest for a Christian ethic invites the question: Which one? The position is further complicated by the existence of a great deal of subsequent Christian literature which enjoys a certain authority. The writings of the Church fathers, of Augustine, Aquinas, Luther, and Calvin, to name the chief examples only, all contain excursions into ethics which arrive at rather different and sometimes incompatible ethical prescriptions. Ethical Christianity tends to ignore this, and when liberal Christians urge us to think of Christianity as primarily a way of life, they do not normally mean to commend the rigors of Puritan morality, though this morality has a clearly established place in the Christian religion and a not inconsiderable basis in Scripture.[2]

On the face of it, then, the idea that we can set out a Christian ethic is implausible. The difficulty might be got round to a large extent, however, by insisting that anything purporting to be a distinctive Christian ethic must be derived from the life and teachings of Jesus in the Gospels. And there seems good reason to accept such a restriction. Nothing can reasonably call itself a Christian ethic which does not, sooner or later, make reference to the utterances of Christ as we have them. Everything else which might claim an important place in Christian ethical teaching is, after all, either intended as a commentary and expansion upon these—the letters of Paul, the theology of Aquinas or Calvin, the deliverances of the Pope—or it is from an external source—the philosophy of Aristotle or Kant, the discoveries of psychology, or the sociology of Marx—which, however helpful, must always be regarded by Christians as, at best, secondary.

The relation between Matthew's and John's Gospel is still something of a problem, but if we do focus on the Gospels as the source of Christian morality there is one obvious place in which this might be expected to be found—the Sermon on the Mount. Indeed, it would not be too much to say that many of those whose views I am here concerned to rebut have in-

clined to the belief that the Sermon on the Mount *is* the heart
of the Gospel, or at least the heart of that Gospel which can
be credible to modern man. And it is upon the Sermon on
the Mount that claims for Jesus as "a great moral teacher" are
most often founded.

But those who make this claim can neither be very clear
about what a "great moral teacher" is supposed to be or have
a very accurate picture of the Sermon. It is plausible to call
Aristotle a moral teacher (whether or not a great one) because
in the *Nichomachean Ethics* he presents an ethic, an account
of how human life ought to be or is best lived, and he gives
reasons for commending it. Socrates too, though in a different
way, is a moral teacher because, at least as Plato represents him,
he subjects certain common and important moral beliefs to
penetrating criticism. One might even think of Confucius in
the *Analects* as a moral teacher, though since it consists in a
collection of precepts with very little connecting or supporting
reasoning, the sense in which he is a *teacher* is unclear. But
the Sermon is nothing like any of these. It is not even a collection of moral precepts. Certainly there are injunctions about
acting which we might call moral, e.g., "If anyone strikes you
on the right cheek, turn to him the other also" (Matt. 5:39 RSV),
though these appear in a section which contrasts them with
precepts like the Ten Commandments, urging us to pass beyond action to motive, intention, and spirit. But equally there
are other injunctions, e.g., "Let your light shine before men,"
that are not obviously moral at all, and the Sermon actually
opens with moralizing of a quite different nature, evaluations
of character—"blessed are the poor in spirit," "blessed are the
meek," "blessed are the merciful," and so on. Now it is important to note that "blessedness" here is a dual notion and contains not only the implication that such people are morally
commendable, but that they are to be envied. The desirability
of their condition lies not in the moral excellence of the actions which flow from it, but that it shall have a reward, a
spiritual reward—enjoying the Kingdom of Heaven, being called
the sons of God, obtaining mercy, and so on. This is a point

to which I will return, but for the moment it is enough to show that the Sermon is not a set of commandments or precepts at all, still less a systemized one.

More importantly, in the Sermon the remarks which refer specifically to what we might think of as moral conduct are outnumbered and take second place to those concerning religious attitudes and duties. The Sermon spans three chapters, Matthew 5–7. The second half of chapter 5 is about killing, adultery, and swearing falsely. It is here that we are instructed to turn the other cheek and to love our enemies. But the next *two* chapters are given over to teaching on religious practices — how to pray, to give alms, to fast, and so on. This preeminence of the religious over the moral is borne out elsewhere in the Gospels, for only a small part of all that Jesus is recorded as having said is expressly ethical, and when he summarizes the Law, the commandment to love God comes before the commandment to love our neighbors as ourselves. If, then, we were to isolate Christ's ethical teachings and give these out as the heart of the Gospel we should have to abandon most of what he says, even in the Sermon on the Mount.

But in fact even this possibility is not really open to us. Any attempt to detach the ethics of the Sermon and forget the theological background destroys the larger part of its *rationale*. If we ask why we should do as Christ commands, the Sermon often has an answer — "I say to you Love your enemies and pray for those who persecute you *so that* you may be sons of your Father who is in heaven"; "Blessed are the poor in spirit, *for* theirs is the Kingdom of Heaven." In these and in other cases the rationale, such as it is, is theological. If we remove it, no reason is given to follow the commands and they must stand as arbitrary.

This conclusion is sometimes disputed on the grounds that it misconceives the nature of the reasons which the Sermon offers. It might be said, on this view, that the rationale we are given for complying with the recommendations is internal not external. That is to say, when the poor in spirit are promised the Kingdom of Heaven, they are not being offered a reward,

the value of which is independent of the goodness of their behavior, a reward which God, quite contingently, connects with
that behavior. Rather, the Sermon invites us to view the poor
in spirit in a certain way and thus come to admire them. Thus,
the rationale for Christian conduct which the Sermon supplies is to be thought of like the injunction 'Be kind, for that
is the centerpiece of morality' and not like the injunction 'Be
kind, for that is the way to attract legacies'.

Such a rejoinder requires examination because as it stands
it is unclear whether or not it conflicts with the position for
which I have been arguing. My argument is that we cannot
divorce the recommendations of the Sermon on the Mount,
some of which we might think of as moral, from the reasons
Jesus gives for endorsing them, and that these reasons employ
peculiarly theological terms. The objection is that this is cir-
cular because the divorce is impossible only if we conceive of
those terms in a supernatural way. But this is not clear. It depends what is meant by "supernatural." Sometimes those who
raise this objection mean to emphasize the truth that the rewards of the Christian life must be conceived spiritually rather
than materially. There is, however, no reason for me to resist
this contention, provided that the contrast between 'spiritual'
and 'material' is conceived in a way that avoids the errors of
Gnostic dualism, a topic to which I shall return at various
points. Alternatively, the suggestion might be that talk of the
Kingdom of God is itself to be understood as a poetic way of
talking about moral purity. But such an analysis, though very
familiar,[3] is either reductionist, and thus not surprisingly makes
the ethical elements in the Sermon on the Mount independent by analyzing the theological language away, or it must
hold on to the indispensability of the theological "poetry," and
hence deny the independence of the ethical. Either way the
view that we can construct a Christian ethic which is independent of Christian theology is not sustained.

A second response to the claim that that pattern of conduct we think of as the Christian ethic must be rationally
rooted in theology or not at all consists in the claim that ethi-

cal Christianity is so plainly good that it will commend itself
to the world without any supporting reason. But I do not think
that this is so. No doubt it commends itself to those who have
commonly been taught its precepts, usually in a properly religious context. But this gives us no reason to expect that it
will be found acceptable to those who have no such background.
Indeed, isolated from Christian theology, there does not seem
a great deal to commend the Christian ethic. We have long
enough experience of a world, in which the weakest generally,
if not invariably, go to the wall and those who go a second
mile will be compelled to go a third and a fourth, to raise a
serious question in our minds as to whether the characteristics
portrayed in the Beatitudes, far from being enviable, are not
a recipe for personal disaster. Moreover, we are inheritors of
Greek as well as Christian moral thinking and generally see
a virtue in taking pride in oneself and standing up for one's
rights. Indeed, as the old Charles Atlas body-building adver-
tisements implied, those who allow themselves to be trampled
upon, used, and humiliated—the meek who turn the other
cheek, in short—are often, and easily, held in contempt by our
common ways of thinking. It is highly questionable, therefore,
whether those important elements of the Christian ethic which
we find in the Sermon on the Mount could or do commend
themselves on their own. At the very least we must say, were
we to ditch the *theological* foundation, we should certainly have
to find some other, and it is not easy to see what it might be.
It is worth noting that those who heard the Sermon were, we
are told, "astonished at his teaching," which hardly suggests
that what was recommended struck them as self-evidently good,
and what impressed them was not the argument or the sub-
lime nature of the precepts, but "His authority." Once more,
then, we must abandon any view of the Sermon which represents it as an elevating moral homily. It simply does not have
this character and what it commends is not concerned with
moral so much as religious conduct. There is no possibility,
therefore, that it could form the basis of an ethical Gospel,
or even that it could supply a morality which we might accept
in isolation from theological belief.

It will be said by some, perhaps, that by concentrating on only certain elements in the Christian ethic—those in the Sermon on the Mount chiefly—I have selected the evidence which best fits my case. Certainly, the ethic that is generally presented as the Christian ethic without supernatural trappings is not so much that of meekness, purity of heart, and so on, as a rather generalized caring concern, which shows itself in kindness, consideration of others, and an anxiety to help the needy. The reason for regarding this as Christian is its place in the New Testament—three places chiefly, Matthew 25, 1 Corinthians 13, and the Epistle of James.

In the first we are told that at the Day of Judgment those who were indifferent to hunger, sickness, loneliness, and imprisonment, whatever their devotional practices, will be cast away from the Father and denied any eternal inheritance, while those who cared for others will be admitted with joy to the presence of God. Now here is a rationale and its essence is this: there will be a final judgment, and whether we like it or not, it is on these terms that the judgment will be made. The fulfillment of all that is important to us and for all eternity will be brought about or prevented in this way. This rationale needs careful treatment if it is not to become a rather unseemly and strictly prudential foundation for doing good, an objection also raised against my interpretation of the reasoning in the Sermon on the Mount. What is needed to save it is the insistence that the eternal inheritance of which Matthew speaks is of *spiritual* value, that is, it is an inheritance valuable to the soul rather than the stomach or the pocket of the individual who seeks it. But however we conceive of the spiritual rewards of heaven exactly, we can see plainly enough that *if* there is a Judge of all things, who is also their creator, with the power and the wisdom to decide our fate for all eternity, we have pretty good reason to pay attention to the terms on which it will be decided. Take away the idea of such a judgment, take away the theology in other words, and all that is left is a picturesque way of making the bald assertion that it is better to care about others than not to do so.

It requires a certain hard-headedness to see that this sentiment, out of a theological context, does indeed require some justification, but it is the case. It is not a belief that has commended itself to all humanity and there are moralities incompatible with it—like the Nietzschean—which make a sufficient case for themselves to put the excellence of caring concern for others to the test. Philosophers know well that it is not easy to defend altruism against the claims of the clear-thinking egoist.[4] Once more, then, we have found that all that is on offer as a Christian ethic devoid of theological overtones is something very general, contentious, needing but lacking a rational basis.

The second passage most often referred to is St. Paul's paean of praise to love or charity. Here charity is said to be chief of the virtues and, because St. Paul had so much to do with the earliest foundations of Christian doctrine, charity is thus considered chief of the Christian virtues. Now I do not especially want to dispute this, but we must ask what exactly the charity is of which St. Paul speaks so enthusiastically and we shall find that this virtue can no more be isolated from a theological context than any other of the contenders for the title of "Christian morality" encountered so far.

St. Paul lists love or charity as one of three virtues, the others being faith and hope. These are not *moral* virtues—like courage or generosity—but religious virtues—like piety and reverence. This alerts us to the fact that charity is commended by St. Paul in this place for being the true way to the end which religious practices seek. It is contrasted not with honor or the pursuit of glory, but with speaking in tongues, prophesying, and martyrdom. In other words, if love is a Christian virtue, which it plainly is, it is as a means of spiritual grace, not as an element of moral excellence. If, therefore, one does not seek, or worse, does not know what it would be to seek, the sorts of ends to which asceticism, religious exercises, and martyrdom might be the means, there is nothing said in 1 Corinthians 13 that gives a rationale for the commendation of charity. Again it might be thought that Paul's picture of love needs no commendation, that his description of it—love is patient, love is kind, love is not jealous or boastful, etc. – is self-commending, but once more I question whether we can agree that this is so. No doubt those who have listened to this passage so frequently read in schools and churches have come to associate it with a glow of general approval, but it is sufficiently natural for Western Christians (as for all people, I suspect) to think well of those who are skeptical rather than credulous, stand up for their rights, and are not willing to take no for an answer for them to question the value of a love that "does not insist on its own way . . . bears all things, believes all things, hopes all things, endures all things." Yet again, therefore, if we remove the theological background, we have lost the rationale for charity's commendation and cannot easily see how it might otherwise be supplied.

The third biblical source to which appeal is often made in support of "religionless Christianity" is the Epistle of James. Here we are told "Religion that is pure and undefiled before God and the Father is this: to visit orphans and widows in their affliction, and to keep oneself unstained from the world" (1:26 RSV), and throughout the Epistle, James is concerned with charitable deeds as the true test of Christianity.

There are, however, two sorts of doubt about appeals to this source. The first concerns its authority.[5] The Epistle of James was not recognized as apostolic by many in the early church and only slowly won a place in the canon. Even then its right to this place remained uncertain. The Council of Trent laid it down as *deutero-canonical*, i.e., of only secondary importance, and Luther would have expunged it from the New Testament altogether, declaring it to be an epistle of straw. Even yet, the authenticity of its authorship and the Christian character of its contents are not universally agreed. It would be highly contentious, therefore, to rely on James, and especially James alone, in support of the claim that Christianity is or can be an ethical faith.

Second, and perhaps more telling, to construe the writer of James as saying that the Christian ethic is independent of or more important than faith in the redemptive work of Christ is to misconstrue him. In the first place the talk of "religion pure and undefiled" is an attack on the value of ritualistic worship, not theological belief, if it is an attack on anything at all. And the celebrated sayings "Be ye doers of the word" (1:22 AV) and "Faith without works is dead" (2:26 AV) must be understood in the light of the purpose of the whole Epistle, which is not to assert the independence of moral conduct and religious faith, but precisely to assert their interdependence. Any faith, James wants to say, which can be divorced from action is the sort of faith which "the devils believe, and tremble" (2:19 AV). That is to say, it amounts to nothing more than verbal assent. We may conclude, then, that neither the Epistle of James, nor Matthew 25, nor 1 Corinthians 13, can provide an ethic any more 'detachable' than the Sermon on the Mount.

I have one further and final objection to the attempt to produce a Christian ethic stripped of supernatural trappings. I have so far been concerned primarily with the first of the two questions outlined at the start—What exactly is the Christian ethic? —and argued that the only possible answer to this question makes it a religious ethic, one that cannot be divorced from the theological concerns of the Gospel. In other words there is nothing that could be set apart as a single code of conduct that would commend itself to ordinary thinking. If we turn now to the second question—What exactly is the Christian Gospel?—it turns out that the best answer to this question contains no explicit reference whatever to those ethical elements that might have formed the Christian code of conduct.

It is now generally agreed that the Gospels as we have them were composed, or at least collated, in their present form some considerable time after the death of Christ, possibly as much as forty years. What they record is that which the early, possibly second generation Christians, thought it most important to record about the life and teachings of Jesus. Consequently they do not contain information on all those questions about Christ that might interest us, nor do they supply a neutral base on which we might construct our own, wholly independent, theological interpretation of his life. Though the fact that they are of this nature does not detract from their value as historical documents, or even as sources of factual information about the life of Jesus, they must obviously be read as they were written, i.e., related and ordered by an independent understanding of the significance of Jesus. What is that understanding? It is to be found most clearly stated in the proclamation or "Kerygma" of the second chapter of Acts.[6] It goes something like this: God's plan for the world, as hitherto revealed in the Jewish Scriptures, has now come to a climax. Jesus of Nazareth was a man marked out wherever he went by exceptional signs of God's power and presence. In the end he was betrayed and killed, but God raised him from the dead, as has been widely witnessed. And this is proof that God has made Jesus both Lord and Christ. To the natural question "If this is so, what are we to do about it?" the same place offers an answer "Repent and be baptised every one of you, in the name of Jesus Christ for the forgiveness of your sins; and you shall receive the gift of the Holy Spirit" (Acts 2:38 NEB).

Now in this answer and the Kerygma which precedes it there is nothing like a moral law, a code of conduct, or even explicit reference to such ethical elements as are found in the Old Testament and the Gospels. Furthermore since, if I am right, we must read the Gospels in the light of this proclamation, its silence on these matters must put such moral instruction as we find in the rest of the Bible in second place to the essential religious message. Are we to conclude, then, that there is no important ethical element in Christianity, and that the essence of Christianity is not concerned with how we ought to live? that there is no distinctively Christian ethic at all?

II

Such a conclusion would be unjustified for four separate reasons. First, there are ethical elements in the Gospels and in the express teachings of Jesus, that is, elements concerned with the conduct of human relations. My claim throughout has been that these cannot be divorced from the theological and religious context in which they appear without serious distortion and loss. But this does not mean that they are not there at all, or may be ignored or forgotten. The important thing is to understand them correctly. Second, the Kerygma presents itself as a fulfillment of the Jewish Scriptures in which a moral law figures prominently, notably in the Ten Commandments. Third, the history of the Christian church can hardly be ignored. Calls to the reform of behavior, even if rarely the chief emphasis, have been an important part of its mission and it would be surprising indeed if these found no basis in Scripture or its collective experience of Christ. Finally, and most importantly in the context of my argument, the proclamation in Acts *does* call for an alteration in behavior — repentance — and without further argument there is no reason to suppose that this will not call into question the character of the would-be penitent's relations with others. But this repentance, which I now want to examine in more detail, must be seen to comprise what is best understood as a religious ethic. This expression, "a religious ethic," is in part intended to signal a rejection of the distinction between 'religion' and 'morality' that has become so familiar in post-Enlightenment thinking.[7] It is an interesting, and in some ways disturbing thought that what the modern world calls 'morality', conceived as something other than law and custom, is a chimera, and while it is the principal purpose of this book to try to understand just what conception of charity has a place in the ethics of repentance, one of its underlying motivations is the belief that the superiority of such an ethic lies partly in the impossibility of *any* religionless morality.

To determine what repentance is we have to look back from the Kerygma to the Gospels. Jesus is presented to us as one who proclaimed the advent of the Kingdom or sovereignty of God. What does this mean? It means first, that He saw, through the apparent reality of the normal and social order, a greater and more enduring order, the Rule of God the Father, creator of all things. It is the will of God which stands in judgment on all things earthly, both contemporaneously and at the last. And Jesus himself, through his complete obedience to that will, will come to be our judge. Indeed, it is the perception that His will is *perfectly* in accord with the Father that leads to the Doctrine of the Incarnation.[8] In Jesus, God offers Himself, sacrifices Himself, and raises Himself for the salvation of humankind. It is this, above all else, which reveals that the abiding principle of the Kingdom is unbounded love, which hates nothing that it has made, and which prefers mercy to justice. Of course, in the Doctrine of the Incarnation paradoxes abound, but I shall not go into the question whether outright contradiction can be avoided. It is enough for my purposes to notice that these paradoxes arise, not from the intellectual gyrations of theologians but from the attempts of the plain men of the New Testament to record their experience and its significance.

The Kingdom of God, revealed by and through Jesus, then, is not to be understood as a world yet to come, though there *is* a world yet to come in which that rule will be complete. The Kingdom of God *now* is partly hidden, but it can be discerned by those with eyes to see, ears to hear, for it breaks through, we might say, in a host of ordinary situations, those situations which Jesus reflects upon in many of the parables.[9] In the light of this Kingdom "types and shadows have their ending" and among these types and shadows are many of the customary religious and moral practices of humankind. The point to be stressed, however, is that this Kingdom is not an alternative code of conduct or system of right and wrong, but is an existing rule—a fact which we can acknowledge or fail to do so. Its impact on morality must lie in the judgment it forces us to pass on the customary attitudes and practices of our society including many of those we call 'moral', and its foundation for such judgments is not that they are better conceived or thought out or something of the sort, but that they are in accordance with the Kingdom of *God*, who made all things and will judge all things.

The question naturally arises as to whether the Kingdom of God really has made its appearance in human history and

whether it is indeed the ultimate reality.[10] It is not the business
of this book to answer these questions, though I shall have
something to say about them later on, but to rest content with
a hypothetical question—If the Kingdom of God has come
among us, if this is a foretaste of the world to come, and if
the proper response to it is repentance on our part, what sort
of charity is rightly thought of as forming an essential part of
this response?

Two fundamental features of the position should be noted.
First, the Kerygma and the Gospels present us with something
that is the case—a claim about how the world is in which we
find ourselves, that it is a world pregnant, we might say, with
the Kingdom of God. Our first response, therefore, must be
an acknowledgment of the truth. (To repeat, I am not concerned
here with whether it *is* true, but only that it is presented as
a truth.) The Kerygma is not a 'way of seeing' the world, or
a code of conduct, but an assertion about what things have
happened and how things are. Second, whatever else it is, repentance must be a free response. In part this follows from the
first feature, for it is logically impossible to compel someone
to believe the truth (a point I shall return to in chapter three).
But it also follows from the fact that repentance must result
in obedience to the will of God, and obeying is not something
we can be coerced or manipulated into. The concept of obedience itself ensures this. To obey a command is not merely
to act in accordance with that command. A dog who is ordered
to cross the road and happens to cross the road at the time
of the order has not obeyed the command. Nor is it enough
merely to comply with the command. People may comply out
of fear of the consequences of not doing so, while at the same
time denying that those whose orders they are following have
any right or authority so to order them. This is the attitude
of most of us to gangsters, terrorists, and invaders, and though
we might call it 'obedience', it ought to be distinguished from
our attitude of obedience to our own laws and legal officers,
which is very different in just this respect. Obedience in the
fullest sense requires on the part of him who obeys not joyful

willingness (which of us obeys the tax laws willingly?) but a
recognition of lawful authority. It requires, in this way, the free
response of a rational agent. Acknowledgment of the rule of
God requires not just agreement that God's commands are such-
and-such, but that they are authoritative, and this is enough
to establish that outward conformity with them is by itself inadequate as a form of repentance.

In the Gospel proclamation, then, the idea that we are confronted with certain very important and inescapable facts and
the idea that we must respond to these appropriately as free
rational agents are of paramount importance. I stress them here
because these two features of repentance carry important implications for any Christian conception of charity, and at the
same time serve to show up the deficiencies in two popular
contemporary conceptions of it. It is these implications and
inadequacies with which the rest of the book is concerned,
but before turning to them, it is necessary to think a little further about the nature of repentance.

If we really are confronted in the teaching and person of
Jesus with the advent of the Rule or Kingdom of God, there
are two different aspects of it that will affect us. The first arises
from the very *fact* of that Kingdom, the second from its special *nature*. This distinction is somewhat factitious, but I have
in mind first that its being the Kingdom of God means that
we cannot, in the end, reasonably hope to ignore it or escape
it, and second that it is the abiding principle of that Kingdom,
love, which determines the precise test by which all conventional convictions and practices are to be assessed.

An instructive parallel here is to be found in the Kingdom
of Satan. Suppose we were to be presented with the claim that
Satan's rule in this world has begun and will come to a full
and final fruition, and were convinced of the truth of this
claim. This alone is enough to raise a question over all our
pleasures and any satisfaction we might take in doing good,
because it is now a possibility that, despite appearances, these
are at best temporary respites from the real horror of things.
But if we were to learn further that Satan were pledged to

maximize suffering we would have reason to harden our hearts sufficiently to allow us to pursue sadistic pleasures, in the knowledge that, so long as we do not enjoy them too much, Satan will sustain them.

This conception of the Kingdom of Darkness is subject to many difficulties analogous to those which Christian theology encounters. I am not here concerned to examine its plausibility (though I believe that those who find the facts of evil a stumbling block to belief in the existence of a good God have reason to take the idea very seriously),[11] but only to illustrate the point that *both* the existence of a judge of all things (whether God or Satan) *and* the nature of his rule (love or hatred of his creation) are involved in the determination of what our response should be. It follows that any exploration of response to God, which following the Apostles we may call repentance, will, in order to discover its distinctiveness, concentrate on the nature of the Kingdom.

According to Christ's revelation many of the customary values of the world are mistaken. It might be supposed that this, if true of the Jewish world in which He moved, need not be true of our world, and is not very likely to be, since our values have been so heavily influenced by the Christian religion. But in fact this is not really so. The values which the Kingdom of God calls into question are still values for us, and I doubt if the impact of acknowledging God's Kingdom is much less radical now than at the time of Christ. What we, no less than the Jews of first-century Palestine, take to be riches are worthless relative to the standards of the Kingdom, essentially treasures which moth and rust corrupt. The Ten Commandments, which have much to commend them, are imperfect and inadequate. Dealing harshly with enemies is mistaken. Even justice which, if anything, is more important to us than to the Jews, is not especially important in the Kingdom of God, for God is to be compared to the owner of a vineyard who pays the same wages to laborers who have done vastly different amounts of work. Those who are anxious about what they will wear or what they will eat tomorrow or the next day and those who carefully guard the little they have rather than risking it in faith are to be condemned. Even adventurers, like the unjust steward, are preferable.

Accordingly, those whom we might think fortunate because able to make the most of life—the happy, the prosperous, the successful—are not actually the most enviable or the most commendable. It is easier for a camel to get through the eye of a needle than for a rich man to live in acknowledgment of the Kingdom, and the truly blessed are such people as the meek, the poor in spirit, those who mourn, since it will be easier for them to accept and live under the rule of God.[12] And so on.

Our first response to this, therefore, must be a recognition that many of the things which we naturally think and do, towards which our greatest efforts are directed and on which our hopes are fixed are mistaken and wrong—wrong because they are contrary to that Will which brought us into being and finds expression in the whole creation, and mistaken because God, though slow to anger, will not be mocked or ignored forever.

Thus "sin" is not primarily an action concept. It does not refer to actions we perform or have performed (an independently implausible interpretation on my view since, though we may all be sinners, it is patently false that we are all perpetrators of equally evil or villainous actions), but rather to our being caught up in a whole evaluative understanding of our lives and the world about us which is deeply mistaken. Sin, we might say, borrowing an expression from Engels, is a sort of false-consciousness of the world and our place in it. It is for this reason that many of the judgments we make of other people and situations are shallow, or just erroneous. When we cast the first stone at others, spot motes in their eyes, reject the women of low repute, or look down on publicans and sinners, we overlook the *facts*. These are not the ordinary, obvious facts however. It would be plain silly to think that all who speak badly of prostitutes are hypocrites because they are themselves prostitutes, and implausible to hold that no one can speak ill of a murderer because he will himself have performed acts that

are just as bad. The fact we overlook is that in terms of the
rule of God, who "hateth nothing that He hath made," and
whose goodness and mercy are unbounded, the distance between the saint and the sinner is not so very great, and without repentance, may be nothing at all. When the two men pray
in the temple and one thanks God for the moral distance between him and other men, his fault is not that his behavior
is unseemly (one ought not to speak too well of oneself), but
that it is foolish, for it overlooks the plain fact that from the
point of view of all eternity he *is* more or less as other men
are. The man who worthily laments his sin and acknowledges
his own wretchedness is not to be praised because he abases
himself and God likes that, but because he acknowledges the
truth.

This aspect of repentance is brought out rather well in one
of Trollope's novels, *The Vicar of Bullhampton*. The vicar and
the local Methodist minister are discussing the case of Carry
Brattle, a "fallen" woman, of whom the minister has been inclined to judge harshly. It is, he says, "a very bad case."

> "And isn't my case very bad" says the vicar "and yours? Are
> we not in a bad way—unless we believe and repent? Have we not
> all so sinned as to deserve eternal punishment?"
>
> "Certainly, Mr. Fenwick."
>
> "Then there can't be much difference between her and us. She
> can't deserve more than eternal punishment. If she believes and
> repents, all her sins will be as white as snow."
>
> "Certainly, Mr. Fenwick."
>
> "Then speak of her as you would of any other sister or brother—
> not as a thing which must always be vile because she has fallen
> once. Women will so speak—and other men. One sees something
> of a reason for it. But you and I, as Christian ministers, should
> never allow ourselves to speak so thoughtlessly of sinners."

When, therefore, deep and strict moral distinctions are made
between individuals, the Christian "sees something of a reason
for it." It is certainly better not to murder, molest, and pillage
than to do so. But though there is this difference, there is, at

another more important level, much less of a distinction between the hardened criminal and the law-abiding, decent, up-
right, prosperous citizen, for both are caught up in a world of
unreality where material pleasures and desires on the one hand
and lawful entitlements on the other loom absurdly large.

III

This way of putting the matter may raise the suspicion that
Christian revelation belittles morality and even puts us in a
world "beyond good and evil," at least as we know it. This is,
it seems to me, a danger in all transcendental religions and
has been widely recognized as such.[13] But I do not think that
it need be so. There can be degrees of depravity, and no doubt
at the bottom will figure many of the horrendous crimes by
which the lives of individuals may be marked. It would be a
mistake, nonetheless, to make 'actions performed' the touchstone of all assessment, or even all moral assessment.[14] Perhaps
we will always want to draw a sharp distinction between the
concentration camp commandant and the ordinary law-abiding
citizen, but this should not blind us to the possibility that ordinary "decent" people may be in a deeper state of moral be-
nightedness than those who have committed crimes. George
Eliot provides us with a portrait of one such person in her novel,
Felix Holt the Radical, in the person of the hero's mother. Mrs.
Holt, seeking the assistance of her minister to deal with her
difficult son, offers him an assessment of her own character.

> "Well, Mr. Lyon, I've a right to speak to my own character; and
> I'm one of your congregation, though I'm not a church member,
> for I was born in the general Baptist connection; and as for being
> saved without works, there's a many, I daresay, can't do without
> that doctrine; but I thank the Lord I never needed to put myself
> on a level with the thief on the cross. I've done my duty, and more,
> if anybody comes to that; for I've gone without my bit of meat
> to make broth for a sick neighbour; and if there's any of the church
> members say they've done the same, I'd ask them if they had the

sinking at the stomach as I have; for I've ever strove to do the right thing, and more, for good-natured I always was; and I little thought, after being respected by everybody, I should come to be reproached by my own son."

When, after more of the same she leaves, Mr. Lyon "walked about again, saying aloud, groaningly—'This woman has sat under the gospel all her life, and she is as blind as a heathen, and as proud and stiff-necked as a Pharisee; yet she is one of the souls I watch for'."

What the episode shows, I think, is that "decent" folk, through their attitude to their own decency, may be as morally unattractive as many of those who commit more obvious offenses. Conversely, it is not so difficult to see how the acknowledgment of sinfulness, while it cannot wipe out past misdeeds, may nevertheless be redemptive. The criminal who sees his crimes, however great they were, in a true light may be in better moral standing than the comparatively innocuous Mrs. Holt. We must understand the human evaluation and the evaluation *sub specie aeternitatis* to move on different, though not wholly unrelated, levels. A parallel might be this. First class passengers may rightly take pleasure in the excellence of their accommodation at the front of the airplane. But if they think that a major part of this excellence is that they end their journey across the Atlantic earlier than those in other classes, their belief, though strictly true, exhibits an absurd misunderstanding of the distance between them and other passengers relative to the distance that all have travelled.

One way of interpreting the parallel is to say that there are two scales of evaluation, good and bad, and good and evil. For the most part, human beings are concerned with good and bad, while the real eternal struggle is between good and evil. It is in general, though not always, absurd to think that "the bad" are significantly closer to evil than "the good." This line of thought needs further elaboration, but it is by the use of some such distinction, I think, that we can see how the Christian revelation may call conventional wisdom into question by throwing it into relief, without putting us beyond what moral sensitivity, on its proper level, regards as important.

A further aspect of repentance, another side to the proper attitude of the penitent, to which I want to draw attention, is its attitude to suffering and evil. If we have clear and authoritative evidence of the final rule of God and if the principle of this rule is His love of His creation, we have reason to believe that all things will work together for good. Christians have never, however, denied the reality of suffering, as certain Hindu and Buddhist traditions do. Indeed it is the fact of human and animal suffering that has traditionally presented the strongest challenge to belief in a loving and omnipotent God.[15] What then is the proper attitude to suffering? The answer is a sort of *via media,* and one that is exemplified in the attitude of Christ to his own suffering, that is, an attitude which while not despairing that good may triumph, neither dismisses nor diminishes the place of suffering in human and animal life. This attitude is both exemplified and *vindicated* in the death and resurrection of Christ, according to the New Testament writers. Jesus exhibits towards his own sufferings and the sufferings of others an attitude which is neither blind submission nor the shallow optimism of 'positive' thinking. It is particularly clear with respect to his approaching crucifixion. "By his Agony and Bloody Sweat" in the garden of Gethsemane, we see that He recognized it for what it would be, a prolonged and immensely painful affair, the best outcome of which would be death, but His "Nevertheless Thy will not mine" exhibits an unshaken faith in the goodness of God, a trust that even this ghastly fate was good if God willed it. Jesus was put to death from a mixture of motives—fear, envy, hatred, and resentment at his disregard for many established and respected ideas, and an understandable anxiety, perhaps, at the social and political consequences of allowing him to continue his ministry unchecked. He was made to suffer both personal humiliation and extreme pain and finally killed. To most minds this is just about the nastiest end a human being can come to, and though we can see a certain heroism in the ability to bow to the inevitable, most of us would think it incumbent upon us to struggle against it with all the strength and intelligence at our command. Now on the Christian view, as I understand it and have outlined it, this is the correct attitude to take. Suffering is hardly ever ennobling and since we are physical creatures, neither wraithes nor angels, pain and death are hurtful to us. But at the same time as struggling against evil we must learn to accept gracefully its temporary success, for if it truly is the case that God rules and his Kingdom is one of love for all creation, these deadly evils cannot prevail. Thus it is only if we cease to believe that God really will make good to triumph, i.e., cease to have faith in God, that we can justify despair.[16]

How do we know that this is the proper attitude to evil and suffering? We know it because we have before us the account of that will which, being perfectly in accordance with God's, undergoes suffering and death. And the result is not that He shows a fine spirit in or attitude to his death and thus overcomes it in some rather precious sense, but that he actually, literally, comes back to life again and comes back *glorified.* Death is shown by the events of the crucifixion and the resurrection not to be the end at all, and this is why the Apostles were so excited and had something they thought worth proclaiming. The resurrection, if it happened, in this way *proves* that God is loving and his love really is supreme. Just what the mode of Jesus' resurrection was is difficult even to conceive, and quite *how* it proves this is also hard to understand. But such, at any rate, it seems plain was the belief of the Apostles, and of those who have celebrated Easter since, and this account of its centrality explains, I believe, why interpretations of the Resurrection which suggest that it did not "really" or "literally" happen have always been resisted.

Christian repentance, then, has these three features. First it acknowledges that our ordinary understanding of this world is quite out of kilter; that the Kingdom of God is a Kingdom of Love, and that it is His love of creation that determines God's will. Second, it expresses freely our desire to get into line with

IMP PAGE

this will, both because we see the paltriness of our own standards and because it is the utmost foolishness to pit oneself
against God. Third, it acknowledges the incipience of the Kingdom, that it is not yet come to fruition and that, in the meantime, the "chances and changes of this fleeting world" must
be dealt with in a manner which at once takes them seriously
and at the same time does not countenance, to the smallest
degree, faithlessness in the goodness of God.

How does this attitude of repentance invoke charity as a
virtue? Let us return for a moment to St. Paul who lists the
cardinal virtues as hope, faith, and charity. We can now see
more easily, I think, how the first two of these are derived. If
"as is most justly due" we ascribe to a God who loves us "all
might, majesty, dominion and power," we have good reason
to regard the future as full of promise, and cannot regard either
our own deaths or the deaths of those we love "as those who
die without hope." And equally, if God is both a loving father
and Lord of all creation, then we can be certain that we are
safe *whatever happens.* Now just how the third, and principal
Christian virtue flows from repentance is not, it seems to me,
so clear. Two things are commonly said—that we must love since
God has loved us; and that since love is the key to the Kingdom we must make it the center of our lives. But neither of
these thoughts makes the connection between repentance and
charity entirely perspicuous and neither says exactly what that
love should be. In the next two chapters I shall be concerned
to show how two common conceptions of Christian love—
psychological healing and the pursuit of social justice—are de-
fective precisely because they cannot be clearly found a place in
the attitude of repentance, and in the fourth chapter I shall try
to ascertain just what sort of charity does have a place there.

IMP
SUMMARY

IV

Before turning to these matters, however, I think it necessary to say something about the rational basis of Christian be-

lief as I have construed it. I shall do no more than make a few observations pertinent to the limited nature of the task I have undertaken.

There is a tendency at the present time, especially among intellectuals perhaps, to suppose that the most important question to ask about the Christian religion is: Does God exist? Some think that if this were answered it would be plain sailing from there on. Either He does exist, in which case we should be Christians, or else he does not, in which case we should abandon religion altogether. In point of fact, however, if this question were settled, it would *not* be plain sailing. Christian doctrine, as expressed in the Creeds, does not contain the proposition that God exists. The Creeds are concerned entirely with His nature and His Incarnation in Jesus of Nazareth. Both of these matters remain to be examined after we have settled (or decided to leave on one side) the question of God's existence.

But even these matters do not encompass the whole area of discussion in which we might engage. Suppose that God exists and that His nature is as Christianity declares it to be. Suppose further that the Doctrine of the Incarnation is true and that at its heart lies a conception of God's Kingdom much as I have claimed it is. Suppose, in other words, that all strictly logical and historical questions can be settled. What follows is the prescription of a mode of existence, a way of living out one's life, i.e., penitently under the kingship of God through Christ. But at this point further questions arise, for we may now wonder, even be led to wonder, whether this manner of life is, whatever its philosophical basis, an acceptable one. It is on this point that I think the limited topic of Christian charity has something to say. And it is a point which may go two ways. Suppose, to the contrary of the first supposition, that we are not persuaded of the truth of the Incarnation. We are nonetheless left with a model of how human life should be spent which may commend itself to us. If, as I have been arguing, it cannot be divorced from the theological conceptions in which it arose, then there is reason, not now of a theoretical kind, to endorse, or better to employ those conceptions. In short, Christianity, as has very often been observed, is a way of life as much as a set of doctrines, and though the falsity of those doctrines would be a reason for rejecting that way of life, given that we must all spend our lives in some way, the desirability of that way of spending one's life would equally be a reason for endorsing the doctrines. It is this two-way traffic that gives the examination of the Christian ethic of repentance its peculiar interest and importance, independently of the philosophical, theological, and historical questions that the Christian religion may raise. Conversely, of course, the undesirability of spending one's life as a Christian might would be a reason to resist any arguments on behalf of Christian theology.

By desirable and undesirable we must mean here personally enriching and impoverishing, where what is in question is spiritual rather than material riches and poverty. At this level we may then raise the question: Is the Christian mode of living enriching? and such a question implies both the question: Does the Christian life lead to joy and peace? as is so often claimed, and if so, Are these the sorts of joy and peace that anyone would find attractive? These questions are, of course, important in themselves and provide a starting point for the next chapter. Here I want to observe only that if repentance with its constituent virtues of faith, hope, and charity *is* enriching, and further, if it is possible only on the assumption of the Kingdom of God, we have an independent reason for believing in that Kingdom. This lends additional interest, it seems to me, to the topics of subsequent chapters, since it enables us to relate the arguments about Christian charity, psychological counseling, and the pursuit of social justice to the wider question of the reasonableness of Christian belief.

CHAPTER TWO

CHARITY AND COUNSELING

Repentance as a way of life is to be commended in part for its rewards. If we ask why we should repent, the New Testament answer is twofold. First, we are sinful—not so much, as I have been arguing, in the sense that we are perpetually performing greater or lesser misdemeanors, but that we are "bound and tied by the chain of our sins" to ways of thinking and acting that are contrary to the ways of God who made us and will be our judge. In a sense this is all the answer we need, for if anyone were to ask why sinfulness is an occasion for repentance, we should have reason to wonder whether his question had any meaning at all. Nevertheless, the Gospel says more—repent and believe and you will be rewarded by the gifts of the Holy Spirit. Whether it would be right to put this in the form "Repent and believe *because* you will be rewarded" we shall have to inquire in due course, but the Apostles and preachers of the Gospel ever since have made it abundantly clear that the gifts of the Spirit which follow true repentance are one of the principal points in Christianity's favor. What are these gifts?

The Holy Spirit, we are told, is a comforter, which means literally one who brings strength, and the forms of his strengthening are love, joy, and above all peace, a peace not of this world, which passes all understanding. This peace, though it flows from a belief that the world of appearances and contingencies in which we find ourselves is neither the ultimate reality nor our final resting place, is valuable, nonetheless, for its making us at home in this world, free from the anxieties and fears which any ordinary view of the world warrants. It is both something experienced and an attitude to the world, a feeling of being secure and a confidence able to ride out the trials and tribulations of this life, even its great tragedies and sorrows. Now it is important to notice that, though this peace is made rational by the belief in the existence of a loving God, the state of mind and the belief are not one and the same. It is logically possible, and not infrequently the case that someone may believe in God's goodness and still be prey to serious fears and anxieties. Such seems to have been the case with Dr. Johnson. Conversely, it is possible to have at least something like the peace of mind of which the New Testament speaks, independently of any belief in loving God. In either case there is a measure of irrationality (viewed from the position of Christian orthodoxy) for in the first the fears are groundless, and in the second the confidence is.

There are a number of implications of this possibility which are of great interest and warrant closer examination. We shall have to touch upon them at a later stage as they are not directly to the point here, which is just that an important part of the Kerygma is its promise of assurance, its promise that in the absence of the visible risen Christ, a holy spirit comes as comforter to all those who truly repent. Indeed, the way the New Testament has it, it is the coming of the Spirit at Pentecost rather than the Resurrection itself which stimulated the development of the church as we know it.

Now there is no doubt that the joy and peace which the Apostles held to be the gifts of the Spirit are blessings indeed. The sorts of fears, anxieties, and unhappinesses to which human beings are prone can, even in the teeth of exceptionally favorable material circumstances, render an individual's life just as miserable as illness and poverty can, and possibly more so. And in a world like the contemporary Western world, in which the sort of poverty that results in perpetual hunger and cold has been virtually eliminated and a very large number of illnesses can be brought under control, these psychological ills have assumed greater importance than ever before. Correspondingly, there has grown up alongside the doctor a considerable army of almoners, social workers, marriage guidance counselors, analysts, and psychotherapists (whom for simplicity I shall refer to from here on as 'counselors') whose business is to bring relief to this type of distress.

Though many, perhaps the majority, of such people have no more Christian inspiration than the average doctor may be expected to, it is not surprising, given the promise of the Apostles, that many Christian thinkers should have supposed that the offer of spiritual wholeness and peace is the most relevant aspect of the Gospel. This has important implications for the understanding of evangelism or Christian mission, for in the light of such a belief the sharing of gifts of the Spirit is *both* the extension of the Kingdom of God into the lives of human beings, *and* an exercise of that love which Christians are bidden to have for their neighbors and enemies, since it consists in working for the greatest benefits they can possess. In this way the duty of every Christian to preach the good news and the duty to show loving concern for others become one and the same.

Traditionally, however, the activities of preaching to one's neighbor and caring for him have been thought to be different, if complimentary, so that any understanding in which they are in fact the same requires us to revise our views of what they are. On this question many people have come to the view that there is much to be learned from non-Christian sources. It is under the influence of this belief that Christian writers and pastors have turned to, among other things, psychoanalytic theory for assistance in understanding spiritual difficulties, and that courses in psychology and psychotherapy have been added to more traditional counseling courses in almost all seminaries and theological colleges. In North America in particular, Clinical Pastoral Education has become a fixed and respected part of the training of the clergy.

There is a danger in such a movement, of course, that the Christian function of the minister or pastor will come to be overshadowed, even eliminated, by these other forms and that he will be converted into just another secular counselor. But most writers on this subject are, it seems to me, alive to this danger and have tried in what they advocate to preserve the identity of the *Christian* counselor. Such attempts may fail, but I am inclined to think that if this were all that is to be said about it there would be no point in saying it again. My criticism runs deeper than this. I shall argue that though it is perfectly acceptable to suppose that Christians, out of charity, must do what they can to "bind up the broken-hearted," there is a certain idea of what we may call "psychological healing," which, whether or not it is Christian inspired, is both morally objectionable and quite inadequate as a conception or expression of Christian charity.

I

My target, then, is "psychological healing" as a conception of Christian charity, but before I begin my examination of it I must make it plain what I am *not* criticizing. I am not criticizing the actual practice of Christian pastors and counselors or even of secular psychotherapists. In the first place I do not know enough about what actually goes on and do not believe myself or anyone else to have sufficient information to make any valuable *general* judgments. Clergy, marriage guidance counselors, social workers, psychiatrists, doctors, and teachers, all of whom may have occasion to counsel, are legion in the Western world and are dealing with case after case. It would be just as absurd to suppose that there is some pertinent criticism to be made of all of their actions as of all the repairs done by garage mechanics in the Western world. Even if one were able to gather information about the thousands of people and places involved (which manifestly one cannot do), so many differences between cases would emerge that no general remarks, commendatory, critical, or prescriptive, beyond those that common sense supplies in any case, would be forthcoming.

Second, I am not criticizing the content or structure of training courses, partly for the same reason as that just given, but also because I know of 'courses' whose sole aim is to effect a greater degree of self-knowledge on the part of counselors and pastors, so that habits and attitudes of which they are unaware do not create unnecessary obstacles in helping those who come under their care. This seems a wholly admirable aim and does not imply any one conception of self-knowledge or any special techniques by which it might be gained.

Third, I am not criticizing theories of pastoral counseling in general. Psychotherapy and the ideal of psychological healing, though they have been very influential, are not the only models of counseling actively promoted or employed.[1] Indeed, there are signs that these are on the wane, even among some of their formerly most enthusiastic supporters, and that more ancient conceptions of the cure of souls have begun to look attractive once more.[2]

This does not mean, however, that my criticisms are of only limited interest. I am concerned with an ideal which has informed not only psychotherapy, but to a greater or lesser degree, most of the writing on pastoral counseling since it came to be recognized as a significant part of theological training[3] and it would be surprising if this did not in its turn mean that the criticisms, if just, have important implications for the content of many college courses and even for the practice of counselors and pastors. My concern, however, is not with these implications but with the ideal itself.

A good many studies have been conducted into the efficacy of psychotherapy and therapeutic counseling. The conclusions of most of these have not been encouraging, but for my part, I am not convinced that the empirical information on success *or* failure can be so easily gathered. This is partly because between what therapists and theorists write and what actually happens there must always be some disparity, since whatever models and methods the theorists of counseling devise and recommend, the counselor on the spot has to apply them under varying conditions and, indeed, interpret them to fit the circumstances in which he finds himself. But it is also, perhaps

largely, because the methods and models of therapeutic counseling that are formulated very often have characteristics that
make their application indeterminate, and sometimes logically
impossible.

Consider this example. In a paper delivered to a Family Welfare Association conference in 1973 on the (then) relatively
new technique of family therapy (i.e., conducting counseling
sessions with the entire family and not just with the individual patient), Dr. A. C. R. Skynner said:

> The model that I tried to develop for myself is not just a tech-
> nique, not something which you can just use like a rule of thumb.
> Rather, I tried to establish a set of principles which would be
> modified according to certain dimensions and parameters, to apply
> to very different kinds of situation. With such an approach it isn't
> just a matter of considering communication or retraining alone,
> or of regression to the point of failure, or facilitating a develop-
> mental challenge, or making the unconscious conscious. It is all
> these different things, at different times, in different relationships.[4]

Now one can understand Dr. Skynner's anxiety to avoid
rigidity in the treatment of patients, but there is a danger, realized in large part in his own case, that too much flexibility will
result in the sort of thing Antony Flew once called "death by
a thousand qualifications." Skynner wants to avoid being confined to a general principle like "focus on the sexual issues or
the Oedipal conflict" and certainly it seems reasonable to suppose that this is not going to be a principle which can be applied fruitfully in every family counseling session. Nevertheless, we must be given some fairly clear guidance about those
family sessions in which it *ought* to be followed. It will not do
to be given principles of the form "Always bear the Oedipal
conflict in mind" for either this tells us nothing about what
we should do when we spot it, or else it requires the incontestable, but wholly unhelpful supplementary advice "Concentrate on the Oedipal conflict when it is right to do so."

The trouble with this principle is not that it is false (I leave
aside the important and complex questions about the psycho-

analytic theory from which such a principle is drawn) but that it is quite worthless from a practical point of view. The phrase 'when it is right to do so' introduces such a measure of generality as to make it impossible to apply without independent guidance on when to apply it. The phrase 'Bear in mind the Oedipal conflict', too, though in its way quite specific, introduces a vagueness which can only be dispelled when we are told precisely what 'bearing in mind' amounts to (and which conflicts are Oedipal for that matter).

Dr. Skynner's lecture is not exceptional. The same feature is to be found in other lectures at the same conference and in countless other places in the copious literature on therapeutic counseling and psychotherapy. One might have supposed, for instance, that the theorist of family therapy is committed at least to the view that it is almost always better (if only for a certain range of cases, perhaps) to interview patients in company with their whole family, even if he is unable to say just what one ought to do in the interview beyond "different things, in different places, in different relationships." But it seems that even this is not so. In a subsequent paper from the same conference proceedings, in which two social workers extol the virtues of family therapy, we find that this method is very flexible indeed.

> When a very significant family member, for example the father or mother, is absent, then the caseworker may be assigned his place, and then we have found that families tend to engage in family therapy more readily.[5]

This seems to amount to the claim that the method of "family" therapy works as well, if not better, when the whole family is *not* present!

No doubt the authors would reply that this does not follow, since by the caseworkers "replacement," the family in the relevant sense is preserved. Leaving aside the fact that such a defense would require the introduction of a great deal of contentious psychological theory and that the business of testing the method's effectiveness is at the least made very obscure thereby, the fact remains that "family therapy" is not what it seems, and that adoption of the method is compatible with *not* getting the family together. Confirmation of this debilitating flexibility comes from another, more recent, source.

In an article advocating the use of family therapy in the case of child cancer cases,[6] two chaplains offer three cases of "the utilization of family therapy theory and technique." In the third case, by their own account, "the meeting was impossible. The father dominated and had answers for everything . . . the daughter would agree with her father . . . the mother and son were very quiet and reluctant to talk. . . . At a later time when the husband was gone, the mother expressed many feelings about her husband. . . . The Chaplain asked if she would bring this up if we met again. She was hesitant but agreed only if the children were *not* present. . . . A meeting was held two weeks later" (my emphasis). To any but the most blindly devoted enthusiast of the technique, this example of its "application" would appear to be its abandonment.

Vagueness and generality under the guise of "flexibility" are, it seems to me, regrettably frequent in a good deal of writing about pastoral counseling, and they can occur even at the most fundamental level. Consider the question 'What exactly is pastoral counseling?' A recent writer gives us what he calls "a working definition which identifies some of the theoretical issues." It is this:

> Pastoral Counselling is a process of interaction between a pastor and one or more persons seeking help with problems they have not been able to resolve with their own resources.[7]

But the generality of this definition makes it worthless. It covers the case where members of a vestry ask their priest for the names of other members of the congregation who might help with the annual jumble sale just as well as it covers any heart to heart talks he might have with members of his flock. It even covers the case of his children asking for an increase in pocket-money to allow them to buy records they cannot afford. Consequently, to assert, for example, that clergy are inevitably involved with pastoral counseling (as defined here) is to assert what is true but empty, and to advocate training courses in counseling might be to advocate anything at all.

Sometimes the generality and vagueness are so very marked that it is hard to avoid the suspicion that the writers concerned do not wish to be committed to anything that might turn out to be wrong. In the United States there is an Association for Clinical Pastoral Education, and one might reasonably suppose that the purpose of such an association would be to promote the cause of one sort of training—clinical training—above other, perhaps more traditional sorts. But even this appears not to be so. In a recent issue of the Association's journal we are told:

> The clinical method as it developed in the modern pastoral care movement literally began in a "clinic" or hospital. As the method developed, the functional meaning of "clinic" has become "real life."[8]

The same writer goes on to identify the "method" as the attempt to learn from experience by reflecting upon it, a "method" that covers just about everything that human beings do from athletics to nuclear physics. Certainly, no one is going to dispute the claim that this "method" is an indispensable part of human endeavor, and *a fortiori* of pastoral and psychological counseling. But this is only because it rules virtually nothing out.

I give these examples as evidence for the claim that the so-called models and methods of modern pastoral counseling are very often so general and/or vague that almost anything may be said to be in accordance with them. This *ensures* that there will be a gap between theory and practice, so that what is said in criticism of the theory need imply nothing critical about the practice. The examples given above, however, suggest that even a straightforward examination of the theory is not possible since it is so often expressed in conceptions too vague to allow critical empirical investigation. And yet it is clear that these and other models and "methods" which writers elabo-

point

rate and practitioners aspire to have a distinctive character and a common basis. The character and basis, however, is not a body of scientific theory which is (as yet) wholly lacking, but an ideal of how the psychological and emotional problems that human beings so often encounter might be dealt with. This is the ideal of psychological healing, an ideal which sees the counselor, despite many differences, on analogy with the doctor, as one possessed of special knowledge and expertise which enable him or her to relieve the mental sufferings of those under care, just as different knowledge and expertise allow the doctor to alleviate and cure physical distress.

This idea is to be found quite explicitly in almost all of the literature on psychotherapy,[9] and is implicit in a great deal that is written on pastoral counseling.[10] In some places, however, subscription to the ideal is uncertain. For example, in a book entitled *Meaning in Madness*, John Foskett records interviews with the mentally disturbed in which the questions and comments of the chaplains are plainly informed by a strong conception of 'healing', whereas Foskett's commentary in the second half of the book regards 'healing' as a limited form of help, possibly because he distinguishes between 'medical' and 'psychodynamical' models of madness.[11] Such uncertainty, it seems to me, arises inevitably from the tensions within the ideal itself as a model of Christian ministry, and part of my purpose is to show this.

I should say at once, however, that subscription to this ideal is not universal. Indeed, in one editorial of the *Journal of Pastoral Care*, entitled "The Secret of Pastoral Counselling," we are told that the rather mysterious nature of Jesus as he is presented in the Gospels

> suggests something important about pastoral counselling. Its ultimate goal is not healing, but revelation. In fact, healing may not be involved at all.[12]

Still, if not universal, the ideal is sufficiently widespread in Christian and non-Christian writings to warrant critical examination.

II

GOAL OF CRITIQUE

Psychological healing has two main features upon which I want to concentrate. First it is therapeutic and second it is, in the language of the trade, non-directive or client-centered. I shall argue (1) that these are mutually incompatible, (2) that the therapeutic aspect is morally repugnant to our common conception of persons, and (3) that the non-directive nature of the ideal is quite incompatible with a belief in the Kerygma as set out in the previous chapter.

Psychotherapy is a talking *cure*. Its aim is not the rational resolution of difficulties through conversation, but the use of talk to effect a cure by the eliciting of underlying causes and, through their exposure, the relief of symptoms. As one writer has it: "Therapy is a talking cure . . . but this is not intellectual talk but Depth talk."[13] The parallel with physical illness and physical cure is plain, and it is this parallel I want to explore for a little.

Doctors are diagnosticians and healers, not scientists. Their ability to heal turns on their ability to diagnose the individual case and to prescribe appropriate treatment. But their ability to diagnose may owe a great deal (and in modern medicine does owe a great deal) to medical science, i.e., the systematic study of anatomy and pathology, and the availability of suitable and effective treatment relies in many cases upon the investigations of physiologists, pharmacologists, and biochemists. Now the practices of doctors, their attitudes and their effectiveness may all be examined quite independently of the science upon which they rely. Conversely, those sciences may be examined independently of their application in hospitals and surgeries. Again, we can subject drugs and other treatments to scrutiny without engaging in any innovative science or concerning ourselves with whether these are properly prescribed in the day-to-day. But all these different facets of physical medicine are held together and make sense only in the context of an ideal — the ideal of healing those who are sick, injured, or who in some other way have malfunctioning bodies.

I have been arguing that, similarly, psychological healing can be examined at a practical level, a theoretical level, or at the level of methods and prescriptions and I have claimed that, as a matter of fact, whatever pastors and other healers may do in practice, they cannot derive much benefit from the "methods" of the theorists of therapy, since these so frequently suffer from a vagueness and generality that makes them logically impossible to apply. Nor, despite the tests referred to earlier, are the methods themselves obviously examinable for efficacy or side-effects, since if we cannot say with certainty whether a method has been applied, we cannot say whether it has been applied successfully or not. What we can say, however, is that the theoretical models *aim* to be something—viz., a method or technique—and this is enough to allow us to think critically about them, because their very intelligibility depends upon the concepts of 'method' and 'technique' being appropriate to that area of human life in which counselors customarily attempt to employ them, whatever the degree of success with which they do so. What most obviously lends itself to examination then is the idea of uncovering the inner workings of the mind and soul in order to devise and develop techniques for alleviating emotional distress and altering abnormal behavior, and to examine *this* we should look more closely at the idea of a technique.

A technique or a method is a repeatable process, which has as its purpose the bringing about of some desired end, and which has a known reliability to do so. Not everything that we do employs a method or technique, even those things which we do frequently and regularly. Breathing, for example, is, in general, not a matter of method or technique—we just do it. Of course, we could have a special method of breathing and some people (opera singers, athletes, fakirs, transcendental meditators) develop these. What makes them methods is that they involve the prescription of a particular *way* of breathing, one which is specifiably different from common or other ways of breathing and which aims at some purpose—the purpose being given by the activity for which the method is intended.

Thus the method "breathing with the diaphragm" which singers employ has as its purpose greater control over the emission of breath, so that it is possible to sustain an even, increasing or diminishing volume over a longish musical phrase. The desirability of being able to do this is given by the activity of *singing* and it is this which makes the method of breathing something worth a try. It is this, too, which makes its effectiveness testable. Such a method of breathing might be (and probably is) quite unsuitable for those who run the 5000 meters.

A method, then, must serve some end. Both the end and the method must be specifiable so that we can make repeated uses of it and check its efficacy as a means to that end. Not all methods are explicitly formulated, however—a pastry cook may employ a method which he cannot actually specify in words—and philosophers have often argued, rightly in my view, that all methods must involve an element which cannot be captured in any verbal formula but must be *shown*, and mastered. But in the main, the use of a method is a self-conscious reflective affair, one in which we can say, if only roughly, what method it is and what purpose it is meant to serve. It is only by being able to say what the method *is* that we can decide whether it works.

It is obvious that the investigations of pure inquiry, whose purpose is not accomplishing any particular practical task, may nevertheless help us to devise better methods of performing them. Anatomical science, by increasing our understanding of the respiratory system, may reveal better ways of breathing for the purposes of singing. And very often science is able to have this useful by-product by first explaining how the method we were originally using works. This, in outline, is the sort of contribution science makes to technology. It is worth observing, however, that we are quite capable of devising useful ways of doing things and even highly sophisticated techniques without any advanced scientific understanding, and that our ability to use some method or other is independent of our ability to explain how and why it works. Thus doctors are often, though not always, well versed in the science that underlies and explains their methods of treatment, but motor mechanics very rarely are. The difference in their knowledge, however, does not guarantee that every scientifically well-informed doctor is a good healer, any more than it prevents a mechanic, who is ignorant of the principles of engineering, from mending a car.

In the light of these remarks let us turn to psychological therapy. I have argued that in the case of psychotherapy and therapeutic pastoral counseling the "methods" of which the theorists speak are far too generally and/or vaguely described to be distinguishable from most of the other things we might try to do in the contexts in which their practitioners are interested. It is easy to *say* that therapy is recourse to a talking cure, one concerned not with intellectual talk but Depth talk, but we have still to be told just what to say—how to talk.

This point is not always easy to see. The attraction of psychotherapy lies in the fact that sometimes talking has an effect independent, apparently, of what is said, and it is tempting to suppose that there is a technique here waiting to be mastered. But the fact itself is a matter of common knowledge. Common experience tells us that those in emotional and psychological difficulty may gain from what we call "getting it off their chests" even when what is said does nothing to alter the conditions that have given rise to the difficulty. Being able to grouse about a difficult relative to someone may help us, even though what is said does not make the relative any less difficult. But to admit this is not to come anywhere near admitting that we have *methods* or techniques for dealing with such difficulties.

The idea that we *have* is fostered by would-be counterparts to medical science, chiefly psychoanalytic theory. I find this wholly unconvincing and do not believe that any of it has ever had a satisfactory empirical basis or undergone any rigorous testing successfully.[14] This is not my point here, however. I want to stress only that the mere existence of a possible theory which, if it were true might explain something of the recognized facts about the value of talk for its own sake to individuals in distress, does nothing to establish the suggestion that there are available, actually or potentially, methods for dealing with psychological distress. *That* claim can only be made good by the specification of methods sufficient for their testing. And I have argued that this is just what psychotherapists and pastoral counselors do not provide.

This is not the only fault, however. The specification of what exactly one must do may be a necessary condition, but it is not a sufficient condition of the specification of a method. We also need to be told what the end in view is and in what context it is to be regarded as valuable. The mere specification of effective ways of bringing about or altering certain types of human behavior does not show that the person who is able to specify these is possessed of any psychological *therapy*. The fact that someone is able to tell us precisely how to engineer some effect in the behavior of some class of human beings is not a demonstration that he is possessed of a therapeutic method. So, for instance, it may be the case (and probably is) that to talk exclusively of sexual desires and conflicts with the recently bereaved is a surefire way to create considerable embarrassment, distress, and offense. It does not follow that, knowing this, we have a therapy for bereavement. Thus far, the "method" is of no greater interest than the "method" of causing spots before the eyes by continuous staring at television.

Now on the matter of specifying precisely what end is supposed to be served by the therapies on offer, those who write about therapeutic counseling tend, if anything, to be even more vague than they are about the precise technique. There is a great deal of talk about helping people to "work through" their problems and of helping them "to relate" to others, and of helping them to "improve their social relations." But such phrases tell us neither what the techniques of pastoral and psychological counseling are aimed at nor what to expect from their use. So debilitating is their vagueness on this point that sometimes it is hard not to suspect the intellectual motivations of those who write on these subjects.

Take, for example, a book entitled *Small Group Psychotherapy*, jointly authored by a number of distinguished psychiatrists. Here is a quotation from its opening paragraphs.

Group psychotherapy has come to be regarded as one of the most important methods for treating patients with emotionally determined symptoms, abnormal behaviour, and personality disorders. Its current position as an effective treatment is based on three contentions: first, desired changes occur more readily with group psychotherapy than with other psychological treatments. Second, such changes are more enduring. Third, people treated in groups improve their social relationships.

Investigators concerned with methods of personality change have postulated that it is easier to alter attitudes of individuals by group methods than by treating individuals separately, and that such personality change will be more persistent. Both these claims can be tested by clinical research.[15]

The first of these paragraphs is rich in ambiguity and vagueness. More importantly, as a consequence of the resulting unclarity the two claims made in the second paragraph could *not* be tested by clinical research, because, on the strength of what we have been told we have no idea what behavior is to count as altered. We cannot say in general when "desired" changes have been brought about until we are told what changes are desired. Nor does it help one to talk of the emotionally determined *symptoms*, *abnormal* behavior, and personality *disorders* for either some highly contentious psychoanalytic theory is presupposed but not made explicit, or else the phrases have no descriptive content whatever. We need to know what behavior is normal in order to know what is to count as a return to normality and we need to know what a well-ordered personality is if we are to spot personality disorders. In this particular book, and in general, these questions are never settled.

Physical medicine, which is the parallel most writers have in mind, can usually (though not invariably) supply these deficiencies in its own case. Just what a disordered liver is, when the heart is behaving normally, and what a malfunctioning eye is are matters for which there are pretty ready answers. The authors of the book I have quoted from might also assert that, though they do not supply them, there are well-established and widely agreed criteria of abnormal behavior and of personality disorder. As a matter of fact I think this is false—and its falsity is demonstrated every time psychiatrists are ranged on opposing sides at criminal trials in which the sanity or normality of the defendant is in doubt. But I do not and need not deny that there are *some* pieces of behavior that are widely and rightly regarded as abnormal *in the relevant sense*, i.e., as suggesting some underlying disorder—obsessive handwashing, schizophrenic changes of mood and attitude, and enuresis are cases in point. What I do deny is that these clear cases amount to more than a tiny portion of the number of different types of case with which psychotherapists and pastoral counselors are typically concerned, and that all highly unusual and undesirable behavior—like gruesome murder and child molesting —is of this kind. If this is so, then the opening paragraphs of *Small Group Psychotherapy* are vacuous.

My purpose, however, is not to attack these particular writers, but to make the general point that before we can sensibly talk of being possessed of therapeutic methods we must be able to specify quite clearly the end which these methods bring about, so that its desirability may be examined. And mere alteration is not evidence of desirability. It must be alteration to the good. Now in the case of physical medicine what the good of the organism is is determined by the functioning of the various organs that comprise it. Physiology and pathology provide us with knowledge of diseases and hence of health, and though there is some uncertainty in some cases (is short-sightedness a disease of the eye or merely a limitation in the power of some eyes?), generally speaking, provided we keep the concepts of health and fitness distinct, physical 'normality' and 'abnormality' may often reasonably be said to be clinically discoverable.

But just what is to be regarded as 'abnormal' or 'normal' in *personality* and behavior is not such a (relatively) straightforward affair. These concepts involve an assumption of *values*, that is, beliefs about what behavior is good and bad, and their proper employment must therefore involve an examination of matters of value. Yet it is just such issues that counselors are anxious to avoid. Some, like those I have quoted, simply fail to tell us what behavior they regard as desirable and why. Others deliberately eschew the question, in the belief that pastoral counseling should be "non-directive." It is this aspect of the ideal of psychological healing that I want to examine next.

III

I have been arguing that the ideas of therapy, method, and technique necessarily imply the idea of a desired or desirable end to be brought about. In some cases this is given by a wider context of activity—methods of training in athletics, for instance, must ultimately result in better times and distances—and in others by the natural functions of objects—the success of methods of curing dyspepsia and trachoma must produce results determined by the functions of the stomach and the eye. In the case of psychological healing, however, just what the end to be achieved is can only rarely be given in these ways. Some of the sorts of case with which counselors and therapists attempt to deal are identifiable psychological conditions resulting in patterns of behavior which are plainly abnormal—like schizophrenic personality disorders or compulsive handwashing —and although, even here, the precise nature of the disorder and just what it is that is malfunctioning is still a considerable mystery to modern medicine, we can allow that it may be possible to establish clinically determinable ends in these cases. But the work of counselors, and with it the idea of psychological healing, extends far beyond these strange and relatively unusual aberrations, and includes bereavement, broken marriages, drunkenness and alcoholism, child abuse, wife-beating, homosexuality, drug-taking, mental handicap, criminality in children, and social isolation. In all of these sorts of case there is no obvious altered behavior which is *the* solution as there is, for instance, in the case of the altered behavior of the schizophrenic.

This does not mean that there are no solutions to these sorts of difficulty, or that no outcome can be shown to be more desirable than any other, but only that just what the end which a therapeutic method should strive for is or ought to be is not something settled, or even something fairly easily derived from a knowledge of the sort of case we are dealing with, but a matter that requires investigation *before* any therapeutic method can commend itself. More importantly, this investigation of ends involves the conscious examination of matters of value.

For instance: no one will deny that wherever there is physical abuse of children by their parents, it must be stopped. But this agreement is not sufficient to allow us to decide between different ways of stopping it. Is it enough that the abuse should be prevented by the forcible separation of parents and children and removal of the children to the care of some other family or institution? Or should we try to engineer the circumstance in which the children remain with their natural parents but are no longer at risk? Many counselors would say that the first solution does not get to the heart of the problem, but to say this is to presuppose that the problem is not just a matter of stopping the physical abuse, but of sustaining the family. My point is that this is so only if the end which any proposed solution is supposed to serve is, or includes, the preservation of the natural family, and this in turn implies that natural family units have some special value. Now this may well be true. Or it may not. In neither case can we deny that this matter of value arises inevitably as we try to choose between methods of dealing with such situations. Thus the investigation of methods implies the investigation of ends which implies the investigation of values.

point

The same point may be illustrated over and over again with almost all the sorts of case with which pastors and counselors deal. For instance, should marriage counselors be aiming—other things being equal—to preserve a marriage or just to minimize the distress caused by its breakup? This question can hardly be settled without serious examination of the value of marriage, for if it is really something of value, there will always be reason to try to preserve it, whereas if it is like any other contract—a matter of convenience to the parties concerned—there does not seem any special reason to do so. So too with bereavement. Those who engage in counseling the bereaved often describe themselves as helping the "clients" to "work through" their bereavement, but it is evident that this description is quite incomplete. What are they to be "worked through" to? In some cultures (including our own until fairly recently) the bereaved are expected to submit to a long period of mourning during which their manner of life and mode of dress are seriously constrained. No doubt those whose affections do not run that deep find this hard to do. Should counselors in such a culture conceive of their task as helping the bereaved to submit to this? Or would "helping" them involve relieving their difficulty by encouraging them to question and reject this severe conception of mourning? The question cannot but involve us in a host of further questions about the value of individuality, social conformity, respect for the dead, and so on.

All those examples are meant to illustrate the point that, just because we cannot divorce the use of any therapeutic methods from questions about the end such methods are intended to serve, so in the sort of cases with which counselors are most commonly concerned we cannot divorce investigation of the end from serious consideration of social and ethical beliefs. Now I do *not* mean to suggest that such beliefs cannot be examined and accepted or rejected on rational grounds, nor that the examination of therapeutic methods in psychological healing cannot be "scientific" because they inevitably involve matters of value which are "subjective." I subscribe to neither view because I believe both to be false. I mean to draw attention only to the fact that questions of social and moral value cannot be *dodged* by the counselor, since without some clear view of what is and what is not valuable in human behavior and human relationships, his conception of a method, whatever it is, is radically incomplete. And yet it is precisely this which the idea of "non-directive" counseling aims to do. For according to the ideal of non-directive counseling, the counselor's own values must be laid aside or held in abeyance in his counseling.

The most celebrated proponent of non-directive, or as its supporters prefer to call it "client-centered" therapy, is the Ameri-

can psychologist Carl Rogers. It would be difficult to exaggerate
the influence his writings have had in both Christian and secular counseling. Rogers presents would-be counselors with a
challenge:

> Are we willing for the individual to select and choose his own
> values, or are our actions guided by the conviction (usually un-
> spoken) that he would be happiest if he permitted us to select for
> him his values and standards and goals?[16]

As the tone of the challenge implies, Rogers believes that the
individual who undergoes "successful" therapy will come to

> perceive himself as the evaluator of experience, rather than re-
> garding himself as existing in a world where the values are inher-
> ent in and attached to the objects of his perception.[17]

Rogers's "client-centered" approach has been accepted and
adopted in a wide variety of places as evidenced by a great
deal of the literature on counseling. One interesting example is a *Casebook in Pastoral Counseling*,[18] which comprises the
reported conversations of American Protestant clergy with
people in varying sorts of distress or difficulty, together with
comments from "experts" after each case. In many of the conversations the pastors are anxious to stress that they pass no
judgment on the behavior of the persons concerned, and on
several occasions the "experts" commend pastors for being "almost wholly non-judgmental." In others they criticize them for
being "too directive." Now if my earlier arguments are sound
it is in fact impossible for the pastors to do anything whatever
to help remedy the situations about which they are consulted,
if at the same time they suspend all thought on what would
be the right solution to them. Equally it is impossible for the
"experts" to comment helpfully on the "methods" of the counselors if they have no views on what they should have resulted
in. Of course, if this is not logically possible, it cannot have
happened, so that what actually goes on in these cases must
be somewhat different to what the pastors and experts think
is going on.

And it is. There are three ways in which the ideal of "non-directive" counseling is unintentionally subverted. First, and least interestingly perhaps, in many cases the pastor just *does* have a view on what should happen and acts accordingly, or he does not and as a consequence recommends and accomplishes nothing. Second, in many cases, the question "what is desirable?" is answered implicitly rather than explicitly by the assumption of the values of philosophical utilitarianism in the rather confused belief, I think, that these are not contentious values. So, in many cases concerning conflict within marriage, the counselor adopts no view on (a) whether marriage as such is valuable and hence whether this marriage should be preserved if at all possible, and (b) which party, if either, is chiefly at fault. He tries instead to relieve the feelings of distress and the occasions of conflict (or at least aims to uncover those things that will do this). In doing so he lends a high value to the happiness of the parties concerned and generally strives for the greatest happiness of the greatest number, i.e., adopts the ethics of Utilitarianism, to the exclusion of any view that says either that marriage is more important than happiness, or that the wrongs of one party against another must be uncovered and righted. (A similar assumption of the utilitarian ethic is evident in the advice given in most agony columns.) Now I do not want to assert here that utilitarianism is false or unsatisfactory (though I believe it is). My point is rather that utilitarianism is itself *an* ethic, so that to presuppose it is not to suspend or rise above ethical questions, but merely to fail to examine them.

It will be said by the proponents of "client-centered" therapy, of course, that there is no attempt to suspend matters of value in their methods, but only an attempt to allow the individual, in Rogers's words, "to select and choose his own values." So, in the *Casebook* I have been referring to, the experts commend the attempt to help clients to arrive at "their own definition" of the problem and its solution. We are told that the good pastor "will not want to . . . impose counselor opinions," and pastoral counseling is contrasted with "authoritarian advice."

Why should we accept this ideal? An answer emerges, I think, when we examine the different, and not altogether compatible, strands of motivation that lie behind the attempt to deal with matters of value in this way. First, there is the idea that objectivity is possible only if the counselor is detached from all matters of value. In the *Casebook*, one commentator thinks it conceivable

> for a secular counselor to take the stance of an impartial scientist not concerned with values. . . . Such a scientist might reason that he respects the right of each person to decide for himself and will not contaminate his free choice by insinuating opinions or prejudices of the counselor into the other person's search for self-affirmation.[19]

This particular commentator, it is true, goes on to wonder whether such detachment is possible for the *Christian* pastor, but he nonetheless holds it out as a *possible* ideal. And yet it is patently absurd. It rests upon the false supposition that matters of value cannot be investigated rationally and impartially. Without this supposition there is no reason to suppose that concern with values jeopardizes impartiality. It is too large a matter to undertake here a defense of the claim that this supposition *is* false, but fortunately it is enough to point out that the same passage which presupposes its falsehood requires its truth. For if there is no discovery to be made by the "counselee" how can he engage in a *search* for self-affirmation? If it is replied that the search is not into a realm of objective value but into his own subjective value, which is already within him but hidden from him by confusion of feeling, this too requires, on the counselor's part, an assumption that self-discovery of this sort is valuable in an objective way. In short, the whole practice of counseling as a means to a better life for the individual, however this life is conceived, presupposes that there are indeed better and worse lives and may not suppose at the same time, therefore, that such judgments cannot be made.

Another tendency which leads to the ideal of "self-direction" (and one also illustrated in the passage I quoted) is the desire not to "impose" values on others. This view, though common enough, is radically confused, for there is nothing in the belief in the objectivity and rational impartiality of ethical reasoning which implies that anyone is to be coerced or imposed upon. Consider, by way of parallel, the reasonings of medical scientists or mathematicians. They assemble evidence in favor of some hypothesis or devise what they take to be a convincing proof. In displaying evidence and proof to other interested parties they are, of course, convinced that the conclusion they have arrived at is correct. This does not mean, however, that they admit no possibility of correction. On the contrary, their belief that there is a truth at stake will make them welcome correction. But none of this implies either that they will want to "impose" their opinions on anyone, or that everyone's opinion on these matters is equally valuable. The belief in the objectivity of mathematical and scientific reasoning carries neither implication. Why then should talk of *moral* reasoning? Of course, throughout history people have wanted to enforce their own moral beliefs and to make the behavior of others conform to them. This is a subject to which I shall come in the next chapter. But this desire, however objectionable, may as easily accompany a belief in the ultimate subjectivity of those beliefs as in their objectivity. There is no logical barrier to imposing my subjective desire on others. It follows that to be persuaded that in most moral difficulties there is *a* right answer which the counselor may be better able to see than those he counsels is not to imply that he has or assumes a right to force them to comply with his conclusion. If, though, he persuades them rationally of the truth of his view, there is nothing in his behavior to be called "imposition." Conversely, to believe in the "subjectivity" of value does not protect us from being coerced into certain ways of behaving.

A third impulse to dispense with the critical consideration of questions of value for the purposes of pastoral counseling comes from the belief that counseling is concerned with the feelings, not the reasonings of the "counselee." But this presents us with a false dichotomy between feeling and reason. What the counselor must decide is what feelings are, in the language of counseling, "negative" and which "positive," in other words, which feelings it is rational to expect, encourage, and promote and which it is rational to discourage. Thus 'feelings' *are* important, but precisely as the subject of rational action on the part of counselor and counseled.

There is, then, no good ground among those most frequently given, or at least hinted at, for anyone engaged in pastoral counseling to suspend his or her own consideration of ethical beliefs in favor of those of the client. Furthermore there are good reasons *not* to do so, reasons suggested both by common sense and by the model of psychological healing itself. First, it is likely that those embroiled in marital difficulties, or who have just given birth to a handicapped child, or whose children have turned to crime are *not* in a good state to exercise the sort of impartiality that moral and ethical issues especially require. This is, as I say, unlikely, even if we were to restrict ourselves to the view of common sense, but if we take seriously the idea we have been considering, that these people are in need of psychological *healing,* i.e., their condition is closer to that of the neurotic or the psychotic than we might be led to suppose by a superficial understanding of appearances, then we would be even more certain that their views on the problems that arise from the position in which they find themselves will be unhealthily distorted.

Second, almost all the situations with which counselors are concerned involve relationships between two or more people, and in many of these relationships feelings are running pretty high and sharp conflicts have arisen, otherwise the counselor would not be involved. In such cases, common sense suggests, it is unlikely that the individuals embroiled in the conflicts will be the best persons to see the overall situation in a balanced and impartial manner, to be able to apply moral rules and concepts judiciously to their own cases. And, for just the same reasons as in the first example, any assumption of the model of psychological *healing* will make this virtually certain.

We may conclude, therefore, that the attempt to subordinate the counselor's rational consideration of moral and ethical beliefs to the opinions of those he counsels is mistaken on two counts; first, it is strictly impossible, since when it appears to happen it does so only because certain value judgments are assumed, and hence not avoided; and second, because, even if it were possible, both common sense and the sort of model of counseling with which I am concerned suggest that it is not a good idea.

I shall come back to this ideal of non-directive counseling a little later on. I have been concerned with it here only in relation to the first of the objectives I set myself: to show that the therapeutic ambitions of counseling and the ideal of non-directiveness are logically incompatible. Since any therapy pre-supposes the idea of a valuable and desirable end to be brought about and since in only a very limited range of cases could these desirable ends be established clinically, counseling therapy can only be developed, if at all, in the light of rationally investi-gated values. Its pursuit, therefore, cannot be combined with the attempt to avoid all questions of value. If therapy is to be possible those values implicit in its endeavors must be inves-tigated. Such investigation, however, raises moral objections to the very idea of therapy itself. Or so I shall argue in the next section.

IV

We have seen that implicit in much that is said by counsel-ors there is the assumption of an analogy between physical and psychological healing, one which puts the counselor on a par with the doctor. I have argued that the exploration of this analogy shows up decided weaknesses in the psychologi-cal parallel. The authors of *Small Group Psychotherapy* say:

> nobody can engage in group psychotherapy without a body of theoretical knowledge, an appropriate vocabulary, and an under-standing of the techniques on which this treatment method is based.[20]

In point of fact, it seems to me, their book goes no distance towards supplying any theoretical knowledge and what they say leaves a very serious doubt about whether they have any method at all to offer, especially since they are crucially vague about the ends any such techniques might be thought to serve. But even if this were not so, even if here and in general we could find applicable methods of psychological counseling, there is a further objection to the analogy. It may be put most simply in this way: people are not bodies and it is wrong to treat them as if they were. To appreciate the full force of this objection, however, we must enter a little more fully into certain topics in moral philosophy.

MORAL CLAIM

There is a distinction, familiar to philosophers at least since Kant, between treating people autonomously and treating them heteronomously. Briefly, to treat people *autonomously* is to treat them as ends in themselves, that is self-governing agents, capable of rationally considered conduct, and thus of deciding and pursuing their own best interests. To treat people *heteronomously* is to treat them as means to ends, i.e., simply as necessary links in a causal chain and valuable for their place in that chain. Rather obviously, both attitudes admit of degree in their formulation and application. Just what it is to show respect for persons as ends in themselves is not easy to say. Some philosophers have even regarded attempts to persuade by demonstrative argument, which might be thought to show the highest respect for others as rational agents, as coercive and hence in violation of the requirement to treat others autonomously,[21] while others have thought that only the crudest treatment of others as objects can uncontentiously be called heteronomous. Neither extreme is realizable in practice, probably. It is difficult to see that social relations between human beings could be wholly devoid of heteronomous attitudes—the employment of functionaries like postmen, for instance, will always involve treating them merely as means to some degree[22]—and on the other hand it is equally difficult to see that we could actually succeed in treating self-moving creatures simply as physical objects for our use—as Alice's efforts to play croquet with hedgehogs and flamingos demonstrate.

Still, if the formulation and application of the concepts of autonomy and heteronomy are unclear, there does seem to be a decided difference of some sort here and one which plays an important part in our moral thinking. Moreover there are some central cases in which the difference is fairly easily discerned. In general, for instance, we treat animals and children heteronomously, believing them for the most part to be subject to the impulsive drive of immediate desires and capable of perceiving and pursuing their own best interests only to a very limited degree, while in general we treat adult human beings autonomously, acknowledging their capacity and hence their right to decide upon and pursue their own conception of the good life. Neither grouping is without exception. Children, after all, are usually on their way to adulthood and will therefore be treated more and more autonomously as they grow older and animals, we are beginning to realize, have a certain autonomy which must be respected. Equally, some mentally handicapped adults can never be granted full autonomy.

In the main, though, adult human beings *are* autonomous, that is, self-conscious, self-determining agents, to varying degrees and ought to be treated as such just because, as in all things, our moral attitudes must respect the facts. To establish respect for persons with this nature as an ideal and an obligation it is necessary to add something about the fundamental equality of human beings, a topic I shall address more closely in chapter four. For the moment, however, I am going to assume, without additional argument, that adult human beings ought to be treated autonomously. In the present context this is a reasonable assumption, I think, partly because it can be found to be accepted by most if not all who engage in counseling, and because under the commoner name "respect for persons" it has such a wide currency in Western thought and practice that the constraints it supplies on the way we treat others are constraints that most people will acknowledge. "Autonomy" is in fact the source of those conceptions of rights and justice which form the basis of most contemporary arguments on social, legal, and moral questions.[23]

I shall work, then, with the assumption that people ought

to be treated autonomously. Two features of this principle are worth drawing attention to explicitly. First, the requirement to treat people autonomously is not the same as that of giving a special place to the interests of others—it is not the same as the Golden Rule (Do unto others as you would have them do unto you). The ideal of autonomy respects the right of each to "go to hell on his own," rather than the interest of each in having a healthy and prosperous life. Consequently, it bids us prefer a world in which some live miserably as a result of their own mistaken choices to a world in which misery is eliminated and the satisfaction of individual desires maximized through the direction of all by the wise. This does not imply, however, that we ought to be indifferent to the interests of others, or that each should be left to fend for himself, but it does mean that there are worse things you can do to others than make them unhappy, and some of these may indeed be ways of making them happy. "The happy slave" is not a contradiction. In fact, this is the second feature of the ideal of respect for persons that I want to draw special attention to. It is, on the assumption that people ought to be treated autonomously, as wrong to use people as a means by manipulating them for *their* own good as it is to manipulate them for *our* own. My contention is that the aspiration of psychological healing is repugnant in precisely this respect.

How, it may be said, could it be thought that pastoral counseling conceived of as psychological healing conflicts with the ideal of respect for persons when (a) it is precisely those who are *not* fully rational with which it is concerned, and (b) it is personhood in the fullest sense that it aims to restore? Now if these claims were true, it would indeed be hard to see that the aspirations of the psychological healer could be faulted in this way. But I do not think that they are. Consider them in turn.

"Counseling," I have already remarked, is a name that covers a professional or semi-professional concern with a very wide range of human "problems." The problems may be divided, roughly, into two sorts—those that involve a malfunctioning

of some kind—depression, schizophrenia, neurosis, psychosis—
and those that do not—bereavement, divorce, family distur-
bances. This division, certainly, does not provide a clear line
of demarcation everywhere. There are many sorts of cases which
do not obviously fall on one side or the other—alcoholism, for
instance—and others about which there is considerable dispute
—homosexuality is a good example. But the existence of contentious cases confirms rather than undermines the suggestion
that there is indeed a distinction to be drawn here. If so, let
us observe that problems on *both* sides of the division may call
forth human sympathy and a benevolent desire to help, since
in all likelihood they will involve personal suffering. Both the
neurotic and the bereaved may be distressed and their families
and friends adversely affected by this. This fact alone, however, does not put them in one category. Both call for help,
but it does not follow that both call for *cure.*

The difference may be said to be this: those cases which call
for cure (neurosis, psychosis, depression, etc.) are conditions
in which the conduct of the sufferer has no rational basis. Those
which call for help, but not for cure, are those in which the
conduct of the sufferer *does* have a rational basis. A couple of
examples will illustrate this. Compulsive hand-washing is prob-
lematic precisely because the sufferers wash their hands when
they have no need to. Someone whose work obliges him to
wash his hands frequently might do so just as many times a
day as a compulsive hand-washer. And the result (or one of
the results)—painfully chapped hands—might be the same. But
the "problems" would be importantly different. In the second
case better hand cream or fine rubber gloves would provide
a solution to the problem because the behavior of the hand-
washer could be expected to alter with the advent of better
methods of doing whatever it is he has to do. In the first case,
though the cream or the gloves might prevent the chapped
hands, neither would be the product of any alteration in the
relevant behavior, precisely because the constant hand-washing
is not a result of a poor method of doing something—it is not
a method of doing anything at all.

Contrast compulsive hand-washing now with bereavement. Here we have, very often, an occasion of great suffering and sorrow. Generally speaking the greater the sorrow is, the greater the affection has been. But this is conduct with a rational basis. It is not only natural but entirely rational to lament a loss, and to lament a great loss deeply. Of course grief may make people ill, but it is nevertheless a mistake to treat grief itself as though it were an illness. What is required in the way of help, if anything beyond human sympathy, is the provision of an understanding by which sorrowers may come to terms with their loss. Well-meaning people often give tranquillizers to those who are sorrowing, but though there may be occasions upon which this is the right thing to do, it is just as mistaken as trying to reason someone out of a broken leg. Very often it is ineffectual because the cause of the grief—someone's death—remains after the effect of the tranquillizers wears off, but this is not the only criticism that is to be made of it. It is also morally wrong. Treating the grief as a piece of abnormal behavior which medication will remedy is no better in kind (though very different in its degree of seriousness, perhaps) than attempts to alter someone's political opinions by admitting him to a psychiatric hospital.

Many people will find this parallel a little hard to accept, but it is nonetheless just. I am not saying, of course, that those who give tranquillizers to the bereaved are just as bad as those who subject political dissidents to psychiatric treatment. But their fault is of the same *sort*. By treating grief as if it were an illness they discount the *meaning* of the subject's behavior and hence regard it, not as the autonomous behavior of a fully human being but a symptom of something else. Paroxysms of grief are very distressing but they are quite different from paroxysms of coughing and no more in need of medication than paroxysms of joy.

To discount the meaningfulness of people's actions and utterances is to treat them heteronomously (that is, as items in a process which unfolds in the way natural processes do) and, viewed in this light their actions and utterances may then be

understood and controlled – though not by the persons subject to them. It is not always wrong to treat human actions
in this way, for some *are* of the right sort (*delirium tremens* is
a clear case). But even where it is right, to do so is to introduce
a distinction between the "patient," who merely undergoes the
process, and the "healer" who controls it. In the psychological
case the division between the two is incomplete. While a physi-
cian may heal himself, since his mental faculties need not be
impaired by his illness, the psychiatrist cannot. In physical
medicine the patient does not cease to be a person because,
though his body is subject to processes he cannot control, he
is not merely his body. In "psychological healing," however, the
patient *is* the person, not his body, and hence if his personhood is subverted, *he* is subverted.

The claims I want to advance are these: (1) It is morally required of us that we treat other people autonomously rather
than heteronomously. (2) There are some cases in which human beings are subject to processes they cannot control such
that autonomy is an impossibility for them unless a cure is
effected. (3) It is vitally important that we be able to distinguish just these cases if we are to avoid subjecting those who
are not ill to "cures." (4) The ideal of "psychological therapy/
healing" inevitably confuses the two sorts of case. The first of
these claims is, as I have said, an assumption I am making,
though on good grounds. The second I take to be the statement of a rather obvious fact, though just how many of the
people who find themselves in mental hospitals are really of
this kind is a hotly disputed matter. The third follows from
the first two, so that the fourth is that which needs defending.

Let me begin its defense by asserting that a perusal of the
literature on pastoral and psychological counseling and psychotherapy will furnish a good many examples of the sort of error
made in the "tranquillizers for bereavement" case. My principal contention, however, is not that such mistakes do happen,
but that the ideal of psychological healing itself induces them.
To put the point simply – if you set yourself to engage not in
"intellectual" talk but "depth" talk, you make it difficult to de-

tect when the "patient" is speaking intellectually. Here is a good example.

> Rita had come to the group with a history of phobias and various physical symptoms, the latter affecting her face and other parts of her body. At the start of the seventh session, Rita indicated that she had a problem she wished to bring up. She then revealed how, to get on in her present job, she had started an affair with one of her bosses three years ago. He was a married man and soon after the affair began she was horrified and guilty at what she had done. When she tried to get out of it the man turned very nasty; he pursued her everywhere and abused her by calling her a whore. This had gone on for the last three years and, though she had tried everything, she could not get rid of him. That very evening he had followed her up to the group; but instead of her usual guilty and persecuted feeling she was seized with anger, slapped his face, and ran into the clinic; and it was from this episode that she was still shaking.
>
> The rest of the group took up her experience with unflagging participation for the next hour. They suggested almost every conceivable possibility of dealing with this man: by getting the police, by writing a lawyer's letter, by telling the manager, by informing his wife, by running away, by getting a psychiatrist to certify him. . . . After some further suggestions, the discussion came to a halt and there was a silence with some signs that members were waiting for the conductor [psychotherapist] to say something.
>
> What was he to say at this point? Several prominent[!] features can be identified in the situation. . . . The external situation in fact derives from a relationship she had endured for three years in spite of her sufferings; the possibility exists that this persecution is something which Rita is maintaining, i.e., it is expressive of a need in her. Rita's hysterical symptoms add further substance to the impression that what she is dealing with is primarily an internal problem. . . .
>
> The conductor . . . commented as follows:
> Rita's problem had preoccupied all the group members but they had dealt with it as an external matter, a view which had not led to a resolution. Because the painful theme of angry feelings to-

wards mothers had come up during the previous two meetings, the conductor wondered if Rita was not expressing a maternal difficulty in her affair . . . was she giving expression to her hating self by identifying with this man and getting him to treat her as she had wanted to treat her mother.[24]

Let us leave aside the contemptibly poor reasoning that this conductor engages in (the sort of thing Anthony Quinton once referred to, in a memorable phrase, as "vertiginous leaps of hypothesis presented as strict deductions"). The point to be made is this. Rita *has* a problem, one which the conductor is pleased to call external, and which the other group members, whose thinking is not as corrupted as his, recognize. She has reacted to it in a natural and rational manner, and could do with some help. But her efforts to make this clear to the group leader will always fail, precisely because he is forever on the look out for deeper "internal" processes, and hence discounts the plain meaning of her words and actions. To this degree he treats her and her concerns as merely the surface indicators of unfolding processes. The same source supplies many examples of the same sort of thing. In another case we are told,

> One man and one woman had met outside the group and were acting out a love affair.[25]

The context makes it plain that the one thing which would never be considered as the explanation of this "interaction" is that the patients were "acting out" this love affair because they were in love. The same systematic reinterpretation not only destroys the autonomy of the patient, it renders the therapist's own conduct immune from rational criticism. At another place we are told that the conductor

> will be more effective in the face of group forces if he has in his therapeutic repertory the techniques necessary for dealing with stressful situations as they arise.[26]

One of these stressful situations is the occasion on which he becomes "the focus of a consensus of negative opinion. . . . The members may share the assumption that the conductor is inexperienced or incompetent." To treat this as a "group force" and seek to employ a "therapeutic technique" to deal with it is, of course, conveniently to set aside the question of its rationality—for *one* explanation of the members' "negative opinion" is that the conductor richly deserves it.

These examples illustrate the way in which thinking about other people's behavior in terms of physical models and "forces" to be understood and controlled amounts to a denial of their status as free human beings. Let me say at once that this may well be done with the best of intentions (though I don't know that it always is), but that this does not make it any less objectionable. It will be replied, of course, that the sort of people who have to seek the help of the psychotherapist are *not* free human beings, that they *are* subject to forces they cannot control. In response I should say first of all that the "forces" appealed to in such cases as Rita's have no empirically well-established foundation whatsoever. Still, it will be said, Rita did have hysterical symptoms, otherwise she would not be there at all. True, but what is supposed to follow from this? Who wouldn't suffer some physical distress in a mess such as she had got into? It has been known for centuries that personal difficulties can give rise to physical ailments, but it is quite illegitimate to argue from this that in such cases the difficulties cannot be dealt with in a rational manner, that "intellectual" talk is inadequate.

What, though, if the "rational" solutions are ineffectual? This is an important point. I want to stress that I am *not* denying that there are such cases. Severe depression hardly ever has a rational basis and it is usually quite fruitless to point out to someone suffering from it that he is in very favorable personal circumstances and that the future augurs well rather than ill. His depression is not a rational response to the condition of his existence and not, therefore, going to be altered by a rational reappraisal of that response. My central contention, however, is that *if* there is no matter about which such a depressive should feel depressed, but his depression persists, it is obfuscating to introduce ideas of unconscious forces which, at one and the same time, both impute and deny rational faculties to him. Rita's case illustrates this. The conductor evidently discounted the idea that Rita's difficulties could be a rational response to the very real existence of her former lover and her fear and hatred of him, and looked instead for underlying "forces," thereby making her behavior non-rational. But the "force" he uncovers turns out to be a different hatred—of her mother— and her behavior a response to this, thereby making her behavior rational at another level. But if fear of her ex-lover is not the whole story, why should her hatred of her mother be? If her response to real difficulties is not to be treated as rational, why should her response to underlying emotions be so treated?

The point is: this sort of psychological healing, far from enabling us to distinguish between behavior which should be treated as autonomous and behavior which should be treated as heteronomous, simply confuses the issue. This is even plainer once we contrast it with psychological medicine of a different order. Depression, I am told, may be caused by a disturbance of those chemicals in the brain which regulate our biological "clocks." If so, there is some hope that eventually we will be able to treat depression effectively either by drugs, or by the simulation of different day and night patterns with artificial lighting and other means. Now here, the behavior of depressives is discounted in the same way as before. Their silence and withdrawal are not attributed to, and therefore not to be understood as a perception that the world is a pretty rotten place. Rather these are treated as a malfunctioning, the result of forces underlying their conduct. The difference is, however, that these forces are physical, the malfunctioning is experimentally ascertainable, and the means used to remedy it do not rely upon the patients' rationality but purely upon known chemical reactions. To adopt physical methods of altering behavior then, though something which may obviously be abused, does not rest upon a systematic confusion of the sort that underlies "psychological therapies."

It will be said, no doubt, that I have condemned a whole range of treatments on the basis of one exposition of a single method. It is true that in this section I have made extensive reference to just one book, but its significance is as an instance of a type. My concern is not with this book so much as the ideal of the psychological therapy which it seems to realize, and this *ideal,* as earlier parts of this chapter are designed to show, is one favored by a good many counselors, the ideal of using *talk* therapeutically. I claim that it is permissible to use *drugs* in this way, in the right sorts of case, but the attempt to use talk in this way simply increases the highly undesirable risk of treating people as means rather than ends in themselves. As I said at the start, counselors cannot actually succeed in using therapies of the kind I have been discussing since none have been developed, but this does not imply that the ideal is not objectionable. Nor does it imply that the conduct of counselors cannot be objectionable on these grounds. As a matter of fact, many counselors and therapists, in pursuit rather than in application of this ideal, do fail in their respect for persons.

V

I have been concerned with an ideal of psychological healing which has the features of being therapeutic and non-directive. I have argued that these two features are mutually incompatible and that the therapeutic aspiration of the ideal is morally repugnant to those who accept, as most of us will, that individuals ought to be respected as ends in themselves. It remains to show that the non-directive, or client-centered character of the ideal is incompatible with the Christian Gospel as set out in chapter one.[27]

Non-directiveness, it will be recalled, is the idea that counselors should not impose their own values on those they counsel. Now the idea of "imposing" values, I suggested, is one which confuses the coercion of another's behavior in accordance with one's moral beliefs with the expression and rational defense of those beliefs. Though I can see good reasons to denigrate the coercion of behavior in accordance with a particular moral code, especially in a pluralist society, I cannot see any objection to the expression and defense of moral beliefs and judgments. Indeed, there may be something objectionable about their suppression. If, for instance, one is called to advise the partners in a marriage which is on the point of collapse through the faithlessness of one partner, it could well be cowardice not to say what one thinks. But there is more to it than this for the Christian, who cannot take the view that evaluative judgments are matters of personal decision or expressions of attitudes which it might be cowardly to disguise, but must hold that behavior and belief are or are not in accordance with the Kingdom of God, and that this is a matter of fact. Furthermore it is a matter of fact which we are well advised to know, since our fate may depend upon it. We cannot repent of behavior or attitudes of whose sinfulness we remain unaware, and to do so may thus be to run the risk of being cut off from God forever. It follows that the Christian counselor cannot do a real service to those he counsels if they remain ignorant of the true relationship between their behavior and the revealed will of God. Whatever else Christians may do they cannot engage in "non-directive" counseling, if this means counseling in which their own understanding of the values involved must remain hidden.

This conclusion may be reinforced in another and perhaps a stronger way. The impulse to engage in counseling, I have suggested, lies in the belief that this is one form in which the Christian's call to charity may express itself. Charity is, at the very least, a concern for the interests of others. Since Christians believe that an eternal destiny awaits us, they must believe that each individual has a major interest in that destiny. If, therefore, there is a right and wrong about our behavior, and upon it our fate for all eternity will turn, anyone genuinely concerned with our interest will not hide this from us. In other words, it could *not*, except in very special circumstances, be an exercise of true charity on the Christians' part to suspend or equivocate about or disguise their considered judgment on someone's behavior.

Why is it that so many well-meaning counselors have fa-

vored the non-directive aspect of the ideal of psychological healing? There are a number of reasons for this, I think, some of
which receive a familiar sort of expression in a celebrated set
of lectures by Dr. C. D. Kean.[28] In setting out the proper role
of the Christian minister Dr. Kean acknowledges that part of
this role must be prophet or preacher, one who "is to present
not his own judgment but God's judgment, as best he can interpret it in the light of scripture and the Church's history, upon
individual and social conditions which seem to deny God's
right to rule. The role of the prophet is always to convict of
sin and point the way to repentance." But he goes on to warn
that the pastoral role must act as an antidote to the prophetic
or the minister "becomes either a scold or a dispenser of mild
moral pep talks."[29] The anxiety that this should not happen
shows itself again in his remarks on auricular confession.

> Any use of auricular confession, within the understanding of
> this approach to Christian faith and pastoral care [i.e., his own],
> will be essentially non-moralistic. Certainly questions of guilt in-
> volve moral considerations, but these are not arbitrary and exter-
> nal in their rigidity, rather they are guideposts along life's way as
> man's moral sensitivity and social experience have developed them.
>
> The approach described here is the opposite from that under-
> lying Roman Catholic theory. . . . The emphasis is on God's prior
> acceptance and forgiveness waiting to be received rather than on
> human guilt.[30]

There are, it seems to me, three strands of thought at work
here, somewhat confusedly expressed. The first may be called
the fear of absolutism. In moral matters, it is often said, there
are no absolutes or, as Dr. Kean has it, moral considerations
are not external in their rigidity, but "guideposts along life's
way." Now what exactly is meant by this is not very clear. Generally it seems to mean that there are no actions or types of
action which are wrong in every conceivable circumstance. Suppose this is true. It would be illicit to conclude from this that
we are never in a position to make unqualified, objectively true,
moral judgments about the conduct of individuals. From the

fact, if it is one, that we cannot declare theft, say, to be always and everywhere wrong, it does not follow that there is always something to be said in favor of any specific piece of thieving. If, then, one is anxious to avoid moral absolutism, one need not renounce a belief in the objectivity of moral judgments. Indeed, it is hard to see how one *could* renounce this. The most plausible alternative to absolutism thus conceived is some form of consequentialism—the doctrine that the rightness or wrongness of an action is to be judged by its consequences. On the consequentialist view, no class of actions can be proscribed *a priori* since any action may have good or bad consequences. Nevertheless, the doctrine implies the objectivity of particular moral judgments since just what consequences an action has is a matter of *fact*. I do not, however, wish to defend consequentialism (which I believe to be false), or, for that matter, to reject absolutism. My point is only that the desire to avoid absolutism, which many proponents of non-directive counseling seem to share, does not actually require anyone to deny that particular moral judgments are objectively true or false, and hence gives us no reason to endorse the ideal of non-directiveness.

The second motivation for this ideal is the desire, so to speak, not to be a moral nosey-parker. To the liberal mind there is something distasteful about pronouncing on the wickedness of others, especially to their faces, and something highly ineffectual about it in those cases where real difficulties have arisen. The contrast is often drawn between helping sinners and preaching at them. Now this view of the matter is largely, I think, a result of popular morality's obsession with sex. The sort of case that those who dislike moral pronouncements have in mind is that of a Victorian, or earlier Puritan moralist who pounces with relish on the fornicator, publicly denounces him, and all in the name of doing him good. What the moralist exhibits, it is said, is an unhealthy concern with the moral condition of others. For my own part I do not think that we should think too lightly of fornication, but it is as plain as anything can be that it pales to insignificance beside the moral turpitude of the

Pol Pots and Hitlers of this world. With these examples in mind, however, the position of the "scold" is quite different. Those who denounce tyrants are often, and rightly, well thought of, and those who fail to denounce them are thought craven, again rightly. If so, the mistake of the Puritan moralist does not lie in his concern with the conduct of others but with being obsessively concerned with one not very important part of it.

It might be said that, if I mean to draw from this piece of argument the conclusion that moral preaching is quite acceptable, I have overlooked an important difference between the two cases. The fornicator and the pornographer beloved of moralists hurt no one other than themselves by their activities. Pol Pots and Hitlers do, however, and this is why they should be denounced. There is, indeed, a point to be made here (about morality and the law), but I do not think it substantially affects what I want to say. There is a distinction, well known to political philosophers, between self-regarding and other-regarding actions, the first being those actions which only affect oneself and the second being those that affect others. Now I am not sure that this distinction, like the distinction between "acts" and "omissions," can actually be sustained, at least to any real purpose, but let us suppose that it can. If the suggestion is that while it is acceptable to concern oneself with the actions of others that hurt or hinder other people but not those that merely hurt or hinder themselves, this is implausible — at least to many people — for there is something to be said in commendation of the person who stops another slashing his or her own wrists, and not just because there may be relatives or onlookers involved. Now why should it be different with those who do themselves moral harm? Suppose that watching blue films or masturbating *is* morally harmful, why would one not at least point this out? We need not take the view (and have reason to reject it, as I shall argue in the next chapter) that the pervert should be stopped if he will not stop of his own accord. Nor need we think it good to denounce him in public, or even that his errors are worth making a very great fuss about (why shouldn't sexual perversions be reckoned just about as harmful morally as smoking two or three cigarettes a day is physically?) In other words, *if* certain practices are detrimental to the subject, and *if* we keep these in true perspective, what is wrong with telling those who engage in them of their wrongness in the right way and on fitting occasions? Nothing, as far as I can see. There seem to be only two possible sources of error. The first is that those who go in for public denunciations have often got the gravity of the offense wholly out of proportion, a point I have dealt with by agreeing; the second is that the practices denounced are quite harmless and hence *not* morally blameworthy. But this objection is of a quite different order. No one need deny that it is foolish to denounce people for practices that are *not* morally wrong, but this hardly establishes that it is wrong to denounce those that are.

The upshot is this: a certain model of the moralizing preacher holds sway over us when we think of moral outspokenness. But it is wrong to think of a concern with the morality of others in this way. Someone might still object to poking one's nose into the moral condition of others on the grounds that it is none of one's business. Here, whatever the secular moralist can think, the Christian must answer thus: it *is* my business, just in the sense that I ought to care what happens to others as well as myself, and what happens to them on the great day of judgment is as real as and more important than anything else that will happen to them. This is a view to which I shall return in the next chapter. My purpose here is just to allay the fear of nosey-parkerdom which lends some support to the ideal of non-directiveness. And this is accomplished insofar as I can show a concern with the moral condition of others to spring from real charitable interest.

The plausibility, and I hope attractiveness, of my view of the matter can in part be brought out by considering a parallel, not that of the doctor and the healing he brings so favored by writers on pastoral counseling, but with the lawyer and the advice he gives. People do get themselves into legal messes, both civil and criminal, and it seems unreasonable to think badly of those knowledgeable in the law and familiar with its processes who offer assistance out of charitable sympathy. Of course it would be intolerable if such people went about investigating the legal standing of others regardless of any evidence of illegality or any request on their part. But there seems nothing objectionable about free law centers where the services of lawyers are made available, and nothing wrong about those who work in them advertising their services and warning people of the difficulties they may get into. (Many existing neighborhood law centers appear to be of this kind.) Consider now the lawyer's relationship to his clients, supposing him to be motivated by a genuine concern with their interests and restrained by a respect for their individuality. He will, without moral repugnance or self-righteousness, tell them exactly how they stand with the law and advise them on how best in his view they can steer themselves through the difficulties in which they find themselves. There need be nothing sanctimonious, no element of the scold in this, but nevertheless the abiding purpose will be to tell the truth and not to disguise the reality of a client's position for fear of making him feel guilty or unhappy.

To my mind this is a much more illuminating and a less objectionable parallel for the Christian pastor to adopt than that of the doctor. I can imagine an important objection to it, however, and one which brings out the third source of the inclination to non-directive counseling. It is the belief in uncertainty, the belief, that is to say, that in moral matters generally perhaps, but Christian morality in particular, just what is and what is not contrary to the will of God is uncertain or even unknown. If this is so, there is this striking *dis*analogy with the lawyer—he has an established body of law to appeal to while the pastor has not. Let us look into this claim.

The first remark to make, perhaps, is that this is a decidedly Protestant view. At one time, of course, Puritans and others were notable for the confidence with which they drew moral implications from Scripture, but Protestantism by its very nature generates disputes and differences and these have not been especially less marked over moral than theological questions.

It is the tradition of canon law that has stood out as a source of clarity and certainty in the promulgation and interpretation of the moral law. Nowadays casuistry has rather a bad name and the moral deliverances of theologians and popes do not have the authority they once had, even among Roman Catholics, but this does not touch the point that the analogy between priest and lawyer will seem highly implausible only to those who ignore an interpretation of the priest's function that has had great influence in a large part of Christendom.

The difficulty, though, for anyone who raises the objection I am considering will not be set aside by the undoubted existence of would-be lawyer-priests. The full force of the objection arises from the skeptical suggestion that, whatever the aspirations of canon lawyers, there *is* no well-established body of Christian moral teaching which can be applied in this way. Now, of course, *if* this were so, the argument would be at an end. But is it? A number of facts are often adduced to support the claim, but these are demonstrably insufficient to establish it. Chief among these is the fact of disagreement. On the questions of abortion, contraception, divorce, and homosexuality, Christians and their church authorities differ. What can we conclude except that there is no one Christian view on these matters? The mere fact of disagreement, however, shows nothing. Scientists disagree, but it would be absurd to argue that there are no true scientific theories. Indeed, it is about the truth of rival theories that they dispute. Similarly, any clear-thinking Christian can claim that differences between Christians show only that some of them at least are in error, not that there is no possibility of truth and error.

But are the disagreements as important as the skeptic suggests in any case? Notice first of all that the list of disputed matters I referred to, which is an obvious list to draw up, shows something of that obsession with sexual morality I drew attention to earlier. That these matters are sources of disagreement is of great importance only if they constitute the larger part of Christian morality. And although the belief that they do is constantly lent support by the public utterances of Christian moralists, radical and orthodox, I should want to question it. (The revival of Just War theory and its application to nuclear deterrence shows, I think, that traditional Christian morality has larger horizons too.[31])

Still, conceding as much as possible to the skeptic in order to produce the strongest refutation of his claims, let us suppose that these questions *are* a large and important part of Christian morality. It still does not follow that there is *fundamental* disagreement among Christians. We need to distinguish between beliefs about what is good and beliefs about what conduct is implied by those beliefs. This is a distinction that tends to be overlooked as a result of another obsession of popular Western morality, the emphasis on behavior and action, morality being commonly thought to consist in principles of conduct to the exclusion of ideals and virtues. Once we employ the distinction it is easy to see that people can subscribe to the ideals and disagree on just how they are to be translated into behavior. Take the case of marriage. No Christian moralist of my acquaintance has disputed the ideal of Christian marriage, that is, the belief that one of the most valuable aspects of human life is to be found in life-long commitment and fidelity to one member of the opposite sex. (I do not mean to imply, of course, that *no* one has disputed this ideal.) In real life, though, marriages do break up, partners are unfaithful, people make mistakes, are attracted to members of the same sex, and so on. Not surprisingly, disagreements arise about how the ideal is to be accommodated to these facts. Some have held that once a marriage is contracted and sanctified and consummated, no Christian should have any part in its dissolution. Others have argued that given certain sorts of marital breakdown, to preserve the marriage bond is at best to preserve a mere semblance of the ideal, and at worst to perpetuate it in a corrupted form. Now my point is not that there *is* one resolution of this disagreement that takes the facts fully into account, preserves the ideal, and is consonant with Scripture (though there may well be), but rather that we can only make sense of the disagreement if we recognize the underlying *agreement* between

the disputing parties. Anyone who thinks that Christian marriage has nothing special about it will not be concerned with
these matters—the dissolution of marriages will not present any
special ethical problem.[32] I do not want to deny that there may
be more radical disagreements than this, but it is my contention that many of the disagreements among Christians on ethical questions will be found to be of this less than fundamental
sort. Consequently the "fact" of disagreement on which much
of the skeptical case rests reveals upon examination a considerable measure of agreement. Connected with this point, it may
be worth mentioning, is the related behavior of others towards
divorcees and the like. One can hold that in divorce something of great value is lost, and perhaps lost by the willful behavior of one of the partners, and hold furthermore that once
a commitment is broken no further commitment of the same
sort can be entered into, and hence no second marriage can
be sanctified in church, without thinking that adultery is an
unforgivable sin, or even a dramatically important one. Still
less need one hold that adulterers and divorcees are to be treated
as outcasts from Christian society. Likewise, if one thinks that
adultery can never be condoned and that the unrepentant adul-
terer is in a state of sin rather than a state of grace, one is not
obliged to make this opinion felt on any and every occasion.
Rather notably, Jesus did not shun the company of men and
women He nonetheless recognized to be sinners—and attracted
exactly the sort of disapproval that many contemporary Christians exude.

I conclude, therefore, that moral disagreements between
Christians are exaggerated and in any case lend no support
to the skeptical contention that there is no common ground
of Christian moral teaching upon which a pastor might rely.
My arguments do not show, of course, that there *is* such a body
of teaching, only that nothing that has been said has ruled
this out. The argument arose, it will be recalled, because of
an objection I anticipated to my suggestion that the lawyer-
client relation is a more promising and illuminating parallel
to the counselor than the doctor-patient one. It is worth point-

ing out now that an objection of the sort I have just been concerned with loses any strength it may have had when employed on behalf of the more familiar medical model of pastoral counseling. For whatever doubts we may have about the existence of sufficiently clear Christian moral teaching to serve our purposes, there can be no doubt, as I have tried to show, that a corresponding body of theoretical knowledge for therapists just does not exist.

Non-directive counseling, then, if I have it right, cannot be a suitable aim for a Christian pastor or counselor. To have shown this is to have completed the last of the three tasks I set myself in this chapter, but the highly negative character of all I have said calls for a more positive conclusion to the chapter.

VI

Theorists of counseling have adopted and promoted the image of counselor as healer no doubt in part because of the very favorable associations which attach to physical healers nowadays. (This was not always so; the image of the doctor up to the middle of the nineteenth century was not very good.) But the associated concepts of healing—diagnosis, therapeutic technique, scientific analysis—are, I have been arguing, (a) unrealized and unrealizable in the real practice of counseling, (b) morally undesirable since they greatly increase the risk of our coming to treat people as objects rather than persons, and (c) incompatible with a commitment to the revealed will of God for the salvation of His creation.

Someone is sure to reply that the theory of counseling is in its infancy; that the sorts of model developed so far are inevitably imperfect; that it is unduly pessimistic to abandon them all on the grounds that none has been successful so far. This sort of response to my argument is quite beside the point. *If models of the kind to which the writers I have made reference to aspire could be devised successfully* (which I do not believe), my arguments show that we ought not to use them, especially if we mean to act out of Christian charity.

Another complaint might be this. Psychotherapists and pastoral counselors are, for the most part, well-meaning people trying to do something in contexts that are almost invariably highly fraught with problems that nearly always prove somewhat intractable. Those, like me, who pour a lot of cold water on their efforts may reasonably be asked what they propose to put in their place, and disregarded if they have nothing to say. The assumption behind this reply is that in difficult circumstances something is better than nothing. Certainly it is true, as G. K. Chesterton said, that if a job is worth doing, it is worth doing badly, but equally the road to hell is known to be paved with good intentions. If a job is done badly *enough*, it is better that it not be done at all, and the best of intentions on the part of those who do it does not alter this.

I want to stress, however, as I did at the outset of this chapter, that I do not mean to criticize the work of those who are, as it were, on the ground. How much or how little good is done in actual counseling sessions, I simply do not know. My criticisms have been aimed at a certain aspiration or ideal, evident in the writings of those who theorize about counseling, though I should be surprised if this ideal had no influence at all on what goes on in counseling sessions, since it has informed and continues to inform a good deal of the training counselors and psychotherapists receive. The mention of training, however, enables us to consider the complaint against me in a more precise form. If counselors should not be trained in the light of this ideal, how should they be trained?

I should say first of all that the talk of "training" is part of the ideal that I want to reject. In itself it implies a schooling in techniques and related theories which, I claim, are neither real nor desirable. In my view, if counselors can be "trained" it is only in the sense that teachers are "trained," a very weak sense indeed. There are good teachers and bad, I suspect, chiefly because there are those who are good at dealing with children and can communicate a real interest in the things they are themselves interested in, and there are those who are not and cannot. Of course, teachers in "training" may learn a great deal that enables them to teach more successfully than they otherwise would have done, but there is no sense whatever, it seems to me, in which a teacher can be "trained" as a plumber is trained. In this respect the doctor is much more like the plumber, while a counselor is much more like a teacher.

None of this means, of course, that we cannot have an ideal of the good teacher to set before those who are learning to become members of the profession. Similarly we can have better ideals with which to inform the studies of those who are learning to become priests and pastors. But if we are in need of such an ideal, there is a traditional one ready to hand—that of the good father confessor. Many Christian churches do not recognize the sacrament of penance, of course, and it can hardly be thought to have much of a place in secular counseling, but it seems to me that the sort of person who will be a good confessor is an ideal there is reason to aim at, whether or not this is associated with a specific rite. And that is a person of strong-minded common sense, high moral sensitivity, wide experience, a secure and unshockable personal character, and deep sympathy with the foibles and failings of humankind. Above all it is important that such a person be able to distinguish clearly between spiritual and psychological turmoil and physical derangement, and to hold fast to moral realities without introducing any element of the prude or the scold.

All this is very well, it may be said, but it does not actually tell anyone what to do when faced with the sort of problems with which counselors contend. It supplies no principles, even very general ones, for the conduct of interviews, for instance, or the analysis of cases. As a remote, somewhat fictional ideal, it may be admirable, but as a training resource it is worthless. This reply raises a still deeper difference between the protagonists of scientific counseling and the view I want to espouse.

I have already alluded to the fact that contemporary Western morality, and hence much contemporary thought about human relations, makes *action* its central concern. Its request is always "Tell us what to do" rather than "Tell us what to *be*." This is a result, at least in part, of the gradual replacement of the moral philosophy of Aristotle with that of Immanuel Kant.

A conception under which the question "How shall I live my life?" is answered with a description of the sort of character I ought to aspire to be, as in Aristotle's *Nicomachean Ethics*, has gradually been supplanted by a conception in which the answer to that same question is given in terms of principles of conduct to which one ought to adhere, such as Kant's categorical imperative or the Utilitarian general happiness principle.[33] Now the investigations of moral philosophers down the years suggest that neither conception is wholly satisfactory, and it may reasonably be thought that there is room in our moral thinking for both. This much is certainly true: there are contexts in which the Aristotelian conception seems to provide a more fruitful understanding than does the Kantian. Counseling, it seems to me, is one such place, a context, that is to say, in which it is better to ask what sort of person a counselor should be than to ask what sort of principles of action he or she should adhere to. It follows that anyone who complains of the ideal counselor I sketched a moment ago, that it offers no principles of conduct, is making demands upon it which are to be regarded as illegitimate from the point of view of the thinking out of which the ideal arises. As a criticism, therefore, it is invalid, unless more can be said at a deeper level on behalf of the demand for principles.

One way of expressing the difference between these two conceptions is to say that the Aristotelian conception makes the idea of *virtues*, states of character, central to its way of thinking about morality, while the Kantian thinks in terms of moral commands or rules of behavior. Accordingly the former will provide analyses of, among other things, attitudes of mind and the nature of the human condition, while the latter will be concerned largely with the intentions and consequences of actions. It is too far beyond the scope of this book to attempt a theoretical examination of the respective merits of the two, or even to wonder which, if either, best fits Christian ethics as a whole.[34] Something more limited might be sufficient for present purposes, however. I hope to show, in chapter four, that we can at least give a reasonably comprehensive and coherent account of charity as a *virtue*, rather than a principle of action, and this is further confirmed by the next chapter which shows, I think, that one such principle "Promote social justice" is not an adequate conception of charity. In the meantime and on the basis of the arguments of this chapter, I feel entitled to conclude that a prominent and popular model of counseling should be abandoned.

CHAPTER THREE

CHARITY AND POLITICAL ACTION

I claimed at the beginning of the last chapter that it is the association of gifts of the Spirit with repentance, together with a concern for the interests and happiness of others that motivates many Christians to examine and engage in "psychological healing," to explore, as many writers avow, the concepts and techniques of psychoanalytic theory and psychotherapy in order to incorporate any insights they may bring into the restoration of personal wholeness. Whatever is to be said for the good that pastors and counselors actually do, I have argued that the ideal of psychological healing implicit in a lot of what is said and written is both self-contradictory and contrary to the Christian Kerygma. Hence no one, especially if his motivation is the Christian virtue of charity, can pursue this ideal or employ the methods it implies. In like manner, I shall argue, those who turn to political parties and ideologies in their pursuit of the Kingdom of God are also mistaken and that this is true whether those parties and ideologies are of the right or of the left. It is the association with left-wing politics which is of special interest, however, because the motivation for it very often arises from a perception that charity bids us be concerned for the interests and happiness of others and cannot be squared with complacent indifference to the poor and the oppressed. It is, I believe, a desire to do something for the poor which underlies the phenomenon called the politicization of religion, a process exemplified with special clarity in the life of the Colombian priest/revolutionary Camilo Torres.[1] For faced with the facts of famine, enslavement, racial discrimination, illiteracy, and so on, many Christians have despaired of ever alleviating the obstacles to God's goodness by means of charitable organizations, however popular and hard working, and looked instead to the organized power of the state to accomplish that which the individual cannot. From this it is a small step to the belief that the structures and processes of the state may themselves need reform, perhaps radical transformation, if the lot of the poor is ever to be remedied. In this way there arises the view that the Christian religion has a political dimension and that the Christian's duty to love his neighbor obliges the church to be involved in politics, whether or not the ecclesiastical authorities think so.[2]

This simple and plausible line of thought deserves close attention. Some of the most influential modern theology is "liberation" theology, and though the writings of many liberation theologians must be understood in the historical context of South America in which they were formed (as many of the writers stress), part of the importance of liberation theology has been its creation of a quite general conception of theology in which there is a large measure of identification with the intellectual analysis, perhaps from a biblical point of view, of oppression and liberation. For many, theology in this identification has finally found its true voice and cast off the irrelevant metaphysical concerns of the past. For others, in this very identification there is exhibited a self-destructive tendency to confuse eternal theological truth with passing political fashion.

This disagreement is hardly new, of course, but it has assumed a new form which is the reflection not merely of different theological viewpoints, but of differences about how those viewpoints are themselves to be formed. To put the matter simply, the dispute is not just about the true social and political implications of theology, but whether the models of thought which we employ in theology, and with them our conception of God, should themselves be formed by social and

political analysis. Thus one of the best-known liberation theologians writes:

> Our purpose is not to elaborate an ideology to justify postures
> already taken, nor to undertake a feverish search for security in
> the face of radical challenges which confront the faith, nor to
> fashion a theology from which political action is "deduced." It is
> rather to let ourselves be judged by the Word of the Lord, to think
> through our faith, to strengthen our love, and to give reason for
> our hope from within a commitment which seeks to become more
> radical, total and efficacious. It is to reconsider the great themes
> of the Christian life within this radically changed perspective and
> with regard to the new questions posed by this commitment. This
> is the goal of the so-called theology of liberation.[3]

In other words, for at least some theologians, theology must
arise from immersion in political struggle, and of course this
view is in sharp contrast to those who think of theology as
an independent inquiry, the results of which must be applied
to and stand in judgment on changing political circumstances.
And yet, it seems to me, the range of conceptually possible
relations between religion and politics is rarely set out or explored in a way which makes this dispute clearly intelligible,
still less resolvable. The consequence, regrettably, is that debate too often does not rise above the level of well-intentioned
sentiment on the one side and bald assertion on the other.[4]

Consider then the line of thought I sketched. No one can
believe that the church or any Christian can with a good conscience connive in the grinding of the faces of the poor for
the selfish material gain of the rich. The question arises, though,
as to why this is wrong. If the *only* answer is that it is contrary
to the Christian religion, there arises the further question as
to whether the Christian can or ought to invoke the collective
power of the state to further the ideals of Christianity, when
the majority of people in most existing states are not Christian and may even be anti-Christian. I shall argue in the first
part of this chapter that Christians ought not to attempt to
do this. It might be replied, however, that defensible secular

goals and Christian ideals come together in this matter and that, while it is his religious beliefs that motivate the Christian, it is secular political argument that justifies him. It is this belief, I think, that lies at the heart of a good many accounts of the possible dialogue between Christians and Marxists. Once more I shall argue that this is not so, for two reasons—first, that the secular conception of social justice which is normally appealed to in this connection is inadequate, and second, that charity can never be conceived properly as recognition of the claims of justice. This is the topic of the second section. Finally, it is sometimes suggested that, though Christianity generates no specific political program and cannot form any but the most temporary alliance with a political ideology, it must nevertheless have what Bishop Sheppard has called a *Bias to the Poor*. In the third section of this chapter, I shall argue that such truth as is in this view in fact leads us away from the idea of political action as an expression of Christian mission or charity.

I

Our first question, then, is whether religious ideals could properly form the basis of the structure or constitution of the state. This is a question of particular interest at the present time, not just in the context of Christian theology and the aspirations of liberation theologians, but also because of the emergence of Islam as a powerful political force in the modern world. The idea of a *Christian* society, of course, like T. S. Eliot's book of that name, is normally associated with right-wing rather than left-wing aspirations. But those who talk about calling into existence a more caring and humane society and suppose, reasonably, that this is a society of which any Christian must approve, are in fact also looking to the idea of a Christian society, a society, that is to say, whose principles of organization are based on Christian values. I shall employ some of the traditional arguments of political liberalism to show that from a political point of view a Christian society, whether of a right- or a left-wing sort, is undesirable. I shall further invoke other aspects of liberal moral thought to show that a "Christian society," thus understood, is undesirable from a religious point of view also.

This is not to say, however, that my argument rests upon the *assumption* of liberal values. I employ the traditional arguments of liberal theory because they are convincing, not because they are liberal. It might be thought, nevertheless, and with some justice, that an exposition and defense of liberal values, and more important, perhaps, of liberal conceptions, is needed in order to allay the suspicion that what is concluded has already been assumed and to provide a convincing challenge to the socialist and Marxist dominated discussion of religion and politics. Such a requirement is reasonable and I shall attempt to satisfy it in the fourth chapter, but I want to stress that the argument of *this* chapter is meant to rely upon its own merits and not upon any prior or assumed agreement on liberal political values.

In the traditional language of political philosophy, the laws which govern our relations one with another are called the terms of civil or political association. It is important to note that civil association is only one form of association in which we find ourselves. We are also associated through families, clubs, and the joint enterprises of businesses, industries, schools, colleges and churches. We may expect, therefore, that the terms of civil association will be and ought to be different from the terms of these other associations. In political society as such, there are rulers and ruled, but no employers and employees, fathers and children, priests and people, students and teachers. Political association has two important features. First, unlike all the other associations in which we stand we can neither grow out of it nor withdraw from it. Association within the family changes as we grow older and sometimes ceases altogether, and there is no club, college, or church which we cannot leave and no business in which we cannot cease to be employed. Second, political association may be and in the main always is an association between perfect strangers. I do not know all the members of my university or of the Anglican communion but I know at least that they all share some common purposes and values; I am, on the other hand, in political association with people of whose interests, aspirations, and capacities I know nothing whatever. If I am involved in a car accident and taken to court by an injured party, laws which are applicable to both of us associate me with someone of whose character and existence I was hitherto quite unaware and to whom I may now find myself having obligations and liabilities.

These facts about political associations are especially important when we set out to consider, as sooner or later we must, what the terms of our association ought to be. In formulating or criticizing the rules of a university or a club it is appropriate to remember and employ a common purpose which it is reasonable to suppose all those who are members will share. In deciding the rules which will constitute relations between, say, teachers and pupils one must consider the end for which they come together, namely education. Now this is just what we cannot do in the case of political association because, since this is an association which necessarily holds between *perfect* strangers, its terms cannot presuppose some particular purpose but must facilitate the pursuit of the most diverse purposes, that is, whatever purpose those of whom we know nothing may as a matter of fact have.

The requirement that political association should facilitate the most diverse purposes paradoxically rules some purposes out. If, for example, to take the most extreme case, my purpose were to destroy everyone else, this could not be permitted by the terms of civil association since this would involve the frustration rather than the facilitating of everyone else's purposes. The example, though bizarre, serves to give us a clue to one general restriction which must govern the terms of our association. Laws must protect those ends and aims which do *not* threaten other ends and purposes from those that *do*. This restriction does not relate only to the destruction of life but also to the theft of property, the use of coercion in the making of contracts, and many other aspects of social conduct familiar to those who read the reports of court cases in their newspapers. I shall refer to all those activities which fall within this restriction as 'legitimate' and those that fall without it as 'illegitimate'. The task of deciding where the line between legitimate and illegitimate falls (a continuous task, incidentally), together with the task of enforcing the distinction, is that which is delegated to the rulers of our association. (It is worth remarking in passing that here a quite separate question arises for political philosophy and for public affairs, namely how our rulers are to be selected, a question independent of the question on what grounds our rulers, however they are selected, are to decide what are and what are not legitimate activities. Democracy relates to the first question, liberalism to the second. On this occasion I am concerned only with the second, but it is important to recognize that the two questions *are* distinct since this opens up the possibility of a democratic regime that is illiberal.)

I have already described one of the grounds upon which the second question is to be decided in fact, by saying that the division must be made in order to effect the protection of all from any. Thus generally expressed I do not suppose that we can derive much concrete guidance on any particular legislative issue. I do not intend to offer a deduction from this general principle to any clear political prescriptions and indeed I doubt whether such can be given, but we can amplify the principle to some point in the context of our interest in religion and politics. First, we may add to it the assumption that no one is above the law so that wherever our rulers draw the dividing line between legitimate and illegitimate activities it is a boundary with which they themselves must live. General opinion in the West at the present time will hardly conflict with this belief but it is worth noticing that no Muslim could deny it either. If the laws we ought to have really are the dictates of God it would be the greatest blasphemy to suppose that the man to whom they are revealed or who is entrusted with their interpretation is not bound by them. The same is true, even, of less emphatically theistic religions like Hinduism. If laws to implement the strict divisions of caste are called for by the proper nature of things the author of such laws is bound by his caste no less than anyone else.

From this assumption the corollary of "mutuality" follows. That is to say, wherever the line is drawn, the activities from which we seek to protect ourselves must also be those from which others are to be protected, so that what we will not allow others to do to us, we cannot allow ourselves to do to them. Conversely, what we wish to remain free to do we must leave others free to do. This applies to the actions of those in political office no less than to those who are not. What we want to be free to use political power to do, we must be prepared to leave others free to do. For example, if we want to use political power to disadvantage (or advantage) some racial or religious minority, the principle of mutuality obliges us to leave others free to do the same, though perhaps they will not choose the same minorities.

In short, political association is an inescapable association between strangers who cannot be presumed to share any particular purposes. It must therefore facilitate diverse purposes, and the rationale of its terms is protection; consequently it requires equality before the law and the principle of mutuality. Let us turn now to religion.

Subscription to religious beliefs has been the cause of a great deal of dissension. We need not hold that differences of opinion are endemic to religion in order to acknowledge that in general, and especially in pluralist societies such as our own, thought and argument about religious doctrines will not, very likely, be productive of widespread agreement. This does not mean that thought and argument on religious questions is worthless, but it does mean that we do well not to rely in practical life upon reaching agreement in such matters. Now some agreement on the terms of our political association, the laws we shall all have to observe and respect, is something we require if civil association is to go on at all. Where there is constant difference of opinion on what the laws should be and how they should be arrived at we have a degree of civil instability which makes the pursuit of life together difficult and at times impossible, finding its logical conclusion as it does, in civil war. These facts, then, present us with a *prima facie* reason for thinking that religious doctrines are not satisfactory bases upon which to found the terms of political association.

This is a point of some importance because those most eager to encourage Christian involvement in politics in the modern world are radically disagreed as to the nature of that involvement and do not realize, apparently, that their call for political action will sanction causes to which they are deeply opposed. So, many who write or speak approvingly and passionately about the need for the church to be involved in politics have in mind only certain select instances. If they speak about Latin America they are thinking of priests who struggle alongside the poor and the oppressed, not of American evangelical missionaries or members of the established Roman Catholic hierarchy whose express intent is to combat communism; and if they speak of South Africa, they are thinking of the clergy involved in the anti-apartheid movement, not those inspired by the traditional thinking of the Dutch Reformed Church. And vice versa. Right-wing Christians will readily denounce the dabbling of left-wing priests in revolutionary activity and, almost in the same breath, call for stricter laws against pornography, abortion, homosexuality, and drug abuse.

The point, of course, is that, although this is often what Christian thinkers *say*, virtually no one actually believes in the involvement of religion and the church in politics *in general*, but only the sort of involvement which will issue in their particular brand of politics. Left-wing Christians do not mean to commend incursions into affairs of state by the Moral Majority, and right-wing Christians do not mean to encourage communistic clergy. It is for this reason that the call for a Christian involvement in politics is in fact divisive, because it can as easily, and perhaps more easily, legitimate involvement on opposite sides of almost all political disputes (witness Northern Ireland and, for that matter, most of the Middle East) as it can unite. If, therefore, we have an eye to practicalities and especially the practicalities of our own time and circumstances, we will see the wisdom of giving a very cool reception to the suggestion that our laws should in any sense be founded on religious doctrines.

These observations, however, are insufficient to establish a theoretical ground for the separation of religion and politics, church and state, because differences of opinion over religious beliefs and their social implications are not logically necessary. People may as a matter of fact all agree. The case of the Islamic revolution in Iran illustrates this for it seems that, at least in the early stages of the revolution, almost all were agreed on the desirability of an Islamic republic and held similar opinions on what this entailed. From this it follows that differences of opinion cannot show religious doctrines to be a *logically* inadequate basis for law only a contingent one. Something more is needed, therefore, and it is to be found in the principle of mutuality elaborated earlier.

This principle has as one of its consequences the further principle that the reason for drawing the dividing line between legitimate and illegitimate activities as we do in any particular case must be the sort of reason which provides a reason to respect the law for all those who must abide by that division. This can only be the case if the division is drawn in order to facilitate all and any of our purposes and not some one purpose which some of us may not share. Now the trouble with reasons which spring from religious doctrines is that they do not satisfy this condition. An Islamic ruler's dictates regarding dress and drink, for example, presuppose not just the truth of Islamic theology, but that all subject to those dictates share the purpose behind avoiding such activities, namely obedience to God. The same presupposition lies at the heart of the Sunday Observance lobby, the Moral Majority, and the Festival of Light. These groups want the terms of civil association to ensure, as far as they can, that God's decree as they understand it is not violated, that God's will is done. Again, those who would have the rich taxed heavily in order to support and increase overseas aid, and who want this not because they see some advantage for all in it but because they understand it to be a social application of Christ's injunction to give all that we have to the poor or to love one's neighbor are trying to establish terms of political association which presupposes some one purpose, the following of Christ, which may not be shared by all those to whom the terms of association must apply. And we should notice that it will not do for them to say, as some of my acquaintance have said, that were they themselves rich they would pay such a tax willingly. This is beside the point. They share that purpose and would, let us hope, *give* that amount of money if they were that rich. What needs justification is their using political power to force others to do likewise.

In contrast to reasons of this sort we may set reasons like the protection of life and the preservation of peace. If the dividing line between illegitimate and legitimate is drawn where it is for reasons of this sort, then the law can be defended in terms of reasons which are reasons for us all, whatever our purposes, since without the protection of life and the existence of peace we cannot pursue any purpose at all.

In short, the pursuit of the life of faith is one purpose that human beings may have. It is not the only purpose and, as the existence of large numbers of secularists demonstrates, it is not one which people do as a matter of fact always have. Consequently, it is not a satisfactory basis upon which to establish the terms of political association. But this is not all. It is the kind of purpose with which some may differ radically. If the religious faith in the ascendant were to enjoin and enforce actions contrary to our own religious or other deeply held beliefs – if, for example, it were to prohibit the worship of Christ, as some varieties of Islam would do, or giving to certain of the poor, as some varieties of Hinduism would do – we should find ourselves unable to comply with the law. This means that we would be *unable* to accept the terms of political association and this is sufficient to show that they are unacceptable as the terms

of an association such as political association is. But this conclusion cuts both ways. It is not the *content* of Islam or Hinduism but the fact that these are religious faiths which makes
them unsatisfactory bases for the terms of political association.
The same may be said for secular ideologies, the most important in the modern world being Communism.

So far I have been concerned with the political side of the
question. My contention is that religious beliefs being the sort
of thing they are, and political association being the sort of
thing it is, religious beliefs are an unsatisfactory basis for the
terms of political association. I should now like to argue from
the religious side of the question, that laws are an unsatisfactory medium for effecting the will of God.

There has always been a suspicion on the part of devout
Christians, I think, that a liberal position such as I have taken
up is evidently right only for those who do not take the claims
of religion seriously. If there really is a creator and sustainer
of the universe who has made His will concerning the social
order plain, there can be no doubt about the moral, prudential, or theoretical wisdom of following it: moral because God
is the fountainhead of goodness, prudential because He holds
the power of heaven and hell, theoretical because His prescriptions spring from a knowledge of the world unique to its creator.[5] If all this is *true* there can be no sense in which the will
of God is an unsatisfactory basis for the terms of political association. Indeed, it must be the most satisfactory.

This is a powerful argument and it does suggest that subscription to liberal political principles is at odds with belief in
God at least as He is conceived in the Jewish, Islamic, and Christian religions. The suggestion may appear to be confirmed by
the fact that the rise of liberalism has been, or at least is widely
thought to have been, coextensive with the decline of religion.
In point of fact the founding father of liberalism, John Locke,
was working within an unmistakably theological framework,
and the country in which liberalism in this respect is most
marked, the U.S.A., is one in which religion continues to attract widespread popular support. But whatever the facts of

liberalism's history, the suggestion that there is some funda-mental incompatibility with religious belief is ill-founded.

In the first place, we can hold firmly to a belief in God, His goodness, power, and authority, and still regard the precise content of His will as uncertain, not from any religious doubt but from a belief in human fallibility. Even if we believe with the major Western religions that God has revealed himself to us (we have not had to seek Him out) that revelation and the interpretation of its meaning come to us through human be-ings. Now it just is a fact that these interpretations, not only between but within the world's religions, are many and vari-ous and this together with the known fallability of human-kind enables us to hold without contradiction that, though we could not do better than base the terms of our political association upon the will of God, this gives us no reason to fasten upon any one interpretation of that will. Such a posi-tion may seem to involve or imply a radical skepticism about the possibility of knowledge of God and hence confirm the devout in their suspicion, but it does not do so. What is doubted is that we can know the will of God both with certainty and with the precision necessary for clear guidance in the business of law-making. For example, we may believe quite firmly that God requires us to honor our fathers and mothers yet remain in doubt of which laws, if any, would be the proper interpre-tation of this requirement. In Calvin's Geneva, it is said, a boy was hanged for failing to show sufficient respect to his parents. It seems reasonable to think one can believe the fifth com-mandment and deny that we should have laws like this.

In the second place, even if we could be certain about the will of God in every detail, it is far from clear that, from a re-ligious point of view, it ought to be embodied in law. The es-sence of political rule is compulsion. It is the business of government to enforce the terms of political association by compelling people to act in certain ways under threat of pun-ishment or penalty. It is in this sense that the law circum-scribes our freedom and for this reason that what laws we have is a question to be treated with the greatest circumspection.

Now there is a conceptual absurdity in supposing, as Aquinas does,⁶ that it is part of the job of the ruler to compel his subjects to act in accordance with the will of God, for if it is the will of God that men should be forced to act according to His commands, He has, if we take the conception of Almighty God seriously, far more ways and better ways of securing this than through what Fitzjames Stephen called the 'rough engine' of the law. This is a more telling argument against the religious use of political power than the first because it turns on the observation that it is just insofar as we *do* take the idea of an omnipotent God seriously that we should doubt the claim that political rule is to be used to enforce His will.

The third argument is more telling still. It concerns a deeper incompatibility between belief in God and the use of political means to enforce in His service. Luther argues in the essay "Secular Authority" that it is logically impossible to force a man to believe since belief requires assent and the most you can force is compliance in what the man says and does.⁷ Perhaps after a time you will, as it were, have made that behavior automatic but there is then a doubt whether it is genuine belief at all. What Luther does not observe is the conceptual connection between belief and action in things religious, a connection which makes absence of assent of a certain kind destructive of the action. For example I might, as the Elizabethans did, force people to go to church, force them even to sing the hymns and say the words of the collects and responses, but if they have neither belief in nor understanding of the nature of what they do, their actions necessarily fall short of worship and prayer. Even if I could and would force the consecrated elements down their throats, this is not sufficient for it to be true that they have taken the sacraments.* "God is a

---

*This might be disputed. Surely, it might be said, orthodox Christianity requires us to hold the sacraments sufficient for salvation in themselves. Luther, for instance, says "the true sacrament . . . does not lose its power on account . . . of impiety and infidelity" (*Sermons on the Catechism* in Dillenberger, *Martin Luther*, 235). The orthodox position is not quite as clear as this suggests, however. It would not be held that a dog

spirit and they that worship Him must worship Him in spirit."
Similarly, if what interests the Muslim is that the will of Allah
should be obeyed, this cannot be accomplished by force because of a logical gap between obedience and mere compliance.
As I observed in chapter one, 'compliance with' becomes 'obedience to' a command not, it is true, through willingness, but
through an acknowledgment that the command issues from
some authority and is performed, willingly or not, because of
that authority. Thus someone who abstains from alcohol or
makeup because the laws of the country prohibit it is not thereby
living a life of obedience to God, but merely to the laws of
the country.

If this is right, we must conclude that the performance of
an act in outward character indistinguishable from an act of
piety may nevertheless be devoid of any religious value. Now
when we incorporate some restriction on behavior or enjoin
some action in the law we will, for the most part, succeed in
making people do as we prescribe. This is not a necessary consequence because, of course, people may break the law. But
in general people, at least in our own society and many others,
obey the law, if only out of fear of punishment. We can thus
ensure that people behave outwardly in certain ways. But this
is not to say that they perform religious acts. Whether what
they do amounts to worship or devotion depends upon what
they believe and in this coercion is powerless. The point may
be made most succinctly in the context of the last example I
gave of actions which some of those religiously motivated have
wanted to enshrine in the law. We can force people to hand
over some part of their wealth or earnings which we may pass
on to the poor, but we have not thereby forced them to give

---

or a baby which had by chance consumed the elements is thereby saved
and no one, as far as I know, has ever thought that the salvation of humanity could be accomplished by the forcible administration of the sacraments universally. Luther in fact says in the same place "When the
minister intones 'This cup is the New Testament in my blood' to whom
is it sung? Not to my dog but to those who are gathered to take the sacrament. These words must be apprehended by faith."

to the poor. It is precisely because they will *not* give that we have taken it from them. Needless to say, still less have we forced them to follow Christ's commandment. In short, their relation to the poor has no religious value whatever, and, I should say, no moral value either. The same may be said about Islam. An Islamic ruler may successfully prevent everyone from drinking alcohol, but he has not thereby made them servants of Allah.

If what I say is correct it follows that those who are concerned to see God's will done can have no use for the apparatus of the state. It may, it is true, be used to increase church attendance, reduce the amount of unsavory literature that is read, make an end to the consumption of alcohol, or increase aid to underdeveloped countries, but it does not thereby bring the Kingdom any nearer. It is worth noting that other things, like social fashions, about which religious believers are less likely to be deceived, may also have these as their effects.

II

My argument so far has been that religious beliefs and doctrines ought not to form the basis of political relationships and that there are both political and religious reasons in support of this conclusion. Those who believe that the Christian Gospel has a social or political dimension, however, may argue that, though Christianity is the motivating force behind their plans for a certain sort of society, the end envisaged and the policies designed to bring it about can in fact be defended on other grounds, grounds which supply a suitably political basis for their recommendations. For instance, to take the case with which I shall be most concerned, Christians are sometimes thought to have a duty to secure a socially just society, but the political justification of such a society (and of any political program adopted with such a society in view) is not that it is in accordance with the Christian Gospel, but that it is a just one. It is in this way, it is said, that Christians may form alliances

with secular political ideologies, for though they seek the Kingdom of God and their allies do not, certain aspects of the Kingdom of God are also things that those ideologies seek.

Such alliances are familiar throughout history. In the early
years of this century they were formed more frequently with
fascist than with socialist parties in the belief that Christians
should join battle against the atheistical forces of Marxism
alongside those to whom, for different reasons, the defeat of
communism was also important. Some of these alliances still
persist, but since the 1960s it is alliances with socialism of one
sort or another that have come to the fore, especially in Central and South America where the theology of liberation has
arisen to give them additional theoretical sanction. These alliances spring from the conviction that the evangelist of Christian love should join forces with the protagonists of social
justice. Thus, Juan Luis Segundo, for instance, equates "the
Gospel commandment to love all men" with the demand "to
seek first justice, before all else, and universal brotherhood,"[8]
and Gustavo Gutierrez sees "liberation" as a correlate of "salvation."[9]

It is not only theologians who have advanced the interpretation of Christian charity upon which these alliances are
founded, but church authorities and their representatives in
many parts of the world. The declaration of the Roman Catholic bishops meeting at Medellín in 1968 includes the statement
that

> Only by the light of Christ is the mystery of man made clear. In
> the economy of salvation the divine work is an action of integral
> human development and liberation, which has love for its sole
> motive. We have faith that our love for Christ and our brethren
> will not only be the great force liberating us from injustice and
> oppression, but also the inspiration for social justice.[10]

In a similar, though slightly more equivocal vein, the authors
of *Faith in the City*, the Report of the Archbishop of Canter-
bury's Commission on Urban Priority Areas (Popular Version),
say:

It is impossible to be a Christian without responding, in one way or another, to the neighbour who is in need. But how? Should this acknowledged duty be confined to personal charity, service and evangelism directed towards individuals? Or can it legitimately take the form of social and political action aimed at changing the conditions of people's lives? These are often presented as alternatives: but in fact a Christian is committed to a form of action embracing both.[11]

The belief is widespread in contemporary Christendom, then, that the aspiration to social justice and a commitment to *caritas*—caring for others—share a common end.[12] As the foregoing quotations demonstrate, just how closely the two are related is a subject on which opinions differ, but several theologians appear to think them identical, and that this identity is biblical. Thus, J. P. Miranda in *Marx and the Bible* says:

> Since at least the sixth century AD a bald fact has been systematically excluded from theological and moral consideration: "To give alms" in the Bible is called "to do justice."[13]

Miranda goes on to cite a few of the passages "which have resisted all misrepresentation." In point of fact the passages cited are not nearly as unequivocal as he suggests, but more damaging to his argument is his lack of clarity about what *modern* conception of justice he wishes to identify the ancient Hebrew and Greek conceptions with. A similar failing is to be found in the use another moral theologian—Robert McAfee Brown—wishes to make of some of the sayings of Jeremiah. To understand Jeremiah properly we have to be clear not only about the Hebrew "sedakah," but about the English "justice."[14]

My purpose in this section is to prize apart the ideals of charity and justice and to show, contrary to this great current of thought, that the traditional Christian duty cannot be construed as a version of this more secular demand. To do so, however, it is obviously necessary to avoid Miranda's mistake and make clear just what conception of justice it is in which we are interested.

In the history of moral and social thought there are at least
two conceptions which are translated by the English word 'justice'. One, that which is to be found in Plato's *Republic,* for
instance, is concerned with the whole range of human conduct, private as well as public. We might, in order to distinguish it, call it 'righteousness' (as, *pace* Miranda, it is usually
translated in the Bible). The second is a much later development in legal and moral theory. It came to prominence first
in the social contract theories of the seventeenth and eighteenth
centuries and as a result of the gradual evolution of European
civil and criminal law. In contrast to the first conception, this
conception of justice applies only to a certain aspect of human
conduct, in general that which has a public character and involves the conflict of interests, and it is closely connected with
the concept of rights.

I do not mean to suggest, of course, that there is no connection between the two. The first is plainly ancestor to the
second, but the second is a much more highly refined notion
and is that which is dominant in contemporary moral and social thought. Its various features will emerge as the discussion
proceeds, but we should begin by noting a distinction within
justice, familiar to political philosophers and legal theorists,
namely that between retributive and distributive justice. The
former concerns the actions of individuals and, more usually,
legal systems with respect to wrong-doers. Anyone who commits a criminal wrong acts unjustly and retributive justice requires that he be punished accordingly. Equally, of course,
retributive justice requires that those who have *not* committed
any wrong must be protected. The principle "the innocent must
not be punished" is as fundamental an element of retributive
justice as the principle that "the guilty ought to be punished,"
and possibly more so.

But there are occasions when questions of justice seem to
arise which do not involve any redress for wrongdoing. The
most obvious of these are distributions. If I am cutting up the
birthday cake at my daughter's party and give the girls much
larger slices than the boys, then, though no question of guilt

or innocence, conviction or punishment arises, it looks as though some question of injustice does, for I have flouted another fundamental principle of justice, namely that "like cases be treated alike." Since, for the purposes of distributing birthday cake, there is no relevant difference between girls and boys, the distribution is unjust.

The idea of *social* justice is really the concept of distributive justice applied to society as a whole and to the comparative positions and possessions of its members. Now it is a matter of considerable dispute among philosophers as to what the principles of social justice are, and indeed whether there is such a thing as social justice at all,[15] but despite this uncertainty it is plain that politicians and moralists, including Christian moralists, increasingly prefer talk of justice and rights to talk of misfortune and charity. This is true even in cases that plainly are misfortunes, like earthquakes, and which do call for charity. The reason is, I think, that "justice," unlike "charity," has a high rhetorical value, in part derived from one of its logical features and in part derived from the "liberal" *mores* of the present time.

This rhetorical value is worth looking at. It is to be observed first of all that claims of justice (and consequent claims of "rights," which share this rhetorical value) justify the involvement of third parties in the way that charity and the duties of benevolence (more properly, "beneficence") do not. For instance, if a wealthy man passes a drunk who, entirely as a result of his own indolence and folly, is desperate for a few cents to get himself a little more of the only sort of satisfaction he can now appreciate, charity or beneficence may be thought to dictate that the wealthy man should give him something. But, if so, the man's charitable duty does not generate a right on the drunkard's part. From the fact, if it is one, that the man ought to give him something it does not follow that he has a right to what he ought to be given. Should the rich man pass by on the other side, the fact that he has not done what he ought to do does not imply that he has violated the drunkard's right. Consequently, we as third parties might think him heartless or simply very mean, but the truth of our judgment upon him does not give us the right to interfere. We would not be entitled to seize his wallet forcibly, for instance, and extract something from it for the drunkard. He has done wrong, we might say, but he has not done anyone *a* wrong.

This is a feature of beneficence in general and charity as one form of it. It may be wrong for me to repay generosity with parsimony or give my close friends very poor birthday presents. But for all this, the generous host has no *right* to a return invitation and my friends have no *right* to better birthday presents. These cases, namely those in which I am or am not beneficent, are to be contrasted with those in which I act unjustly. Suppose the rich man does give the drunkard a couple of dollars and someone else, on the true but inadequate ground that the money will merely go on more drink, takes it away again. He believes that the rich man did wrong to give it, no doubt, but even if he is correct in this belief, he does not have the right to take it away. The money, for good or ill, has been given to the drunkard and is his. It is his *now,* by right. Consequently, a policeman or any third party, who would have had no right to transfer the money from the rich man to the beggar in the first place, does have a right to transfer it back to the beggar. The point is: though it was not his by right before he was given it (even though he ought to have been given it), having been given it, it is his by right. Third parties, when they insist upon the rights of others, act justly. But they do not act justly when they try to bring about the same material result (two dollars in the pocket of the drunkard) without that right.

It should be plain enough in the light of these remarks why there is moral and rhetorical value in construing distribution as a matter of justice. Many people across the world live in abject poverty. They do not, by and large, rise up and seize the goods of the rich, and the rich, by and large, pass by on the other side. If those who want to end this abject poverty also have the power to seize the goods of the rich (or a reasonable portion of them) they can rightfully do so if the condition of the poor is one of injustice, not if it is not. If the poor have a *right* to a larger share of the world's goods than they actually enjoy, anyone who seizes it on their behalf is not engaged in stealing but in restitution and thus promoting, not subverting, justice. But if the poor do not have a right, only a *need* for assistance, their appeal must be to the benevolence of the rich, and if this appeal goes unheard for the most part, third parties must content themselves with deploring the heartlessness of the rich.

The second source of rhetorical value in talk of justice lies in one contemporary legacy of liberalism. Why is it, one might wonder, that many good causes prefer to talk in terms of rights rather than needs? The answer is that it is thought (erroneously, I shall argue in the next chapter) that to be dependent upon the benevolence of others for what one needs is an affront to human dignity. In our common moral consciousness justice and rights form the basis of most appeals by self-respecting adult individuals, needs and wants the basis of appeals in childhood. To acknowledge a need or desire for charity is to confess an inadequacy, a lack of that self-reliance which is an important part of the ideal of autonomy at the heart of liberal individualism. It is this that has given "charity" a bad name and persuaded well-meaning people to speak (confusedly) of rights and justice instead. But unlike the implication for third parties, this feature of justice is, in my view, not a necessary but a purely contingent one and, as I shall try to show later on, there is, for the Christian at any rate, a deep sense of equal worth with which the demands and practice of charity not only do not conflict but which, in a sense, they express. (It may be worth remarking in passing on the irony that it is socialist writers who rely heavily on the rhetorical value of "social justice," while at the same time denying the ideal of the self-reliant autonomous individual upon which it rests in favor of some communitarian ideal.)

Construing the world's ills in terms of rights and social justice, then, has rhetorical value and this being so it is easy to see (a) why people concerned with poverty and deprivation talk in this way and (b) that the fact that they do so does not in itself show the foundations of their moral view to be sound. That is to say, there are good reasons for talking about justice and rights in preference to needs and charity—it is more effective in contemporary debate—and for this reason many people speak in this way. But it does not follow that they are right to do so. The task of this section is to show that they are *not*, and in the next (and final) chapter, I hope to restore some rhetorical value to the concept of charity by showing that it is, in fact, the more admirable ideal.

The context in which I shall discuss these questions is world poverty and the relations between rich and poor both as nations and as individuals.[16] It is here that some of the most famous "charities" operate and here that the problems are most often conceived in terms of rights and justice. But before any moral implications can be drawn from the facts, the facts must be established. Commonly three assumptions are made by Christian and other writers on third world poverty. First, that there is a very great deal of hunger, disease, death, and homelessness in the world, and that the situation is deteriorating. Second, that a more equal distribution of private and collective wealth across the globe, if it would not obliterate, would certainly do much to remedy third world distress. Third, that the present deplorable condition has arisen in large part from the past actions of colonialists, that is, the past actions of those nations whose populations are now rich against those nations whose populations are now poor. It is less commonly observed that all three of these claims are highly contentious and at best extremely hard to establish.

In the case of the first, the problem is chiefly one of information gathering. Although it is often said, for instance, that "every minute of every day thirty people in the world die of hunger and hunger-related diseases,"[17] those whose professional concern is with social statistics know that it is impossible to arrive at such a precise figure with any certainty. Notoriously, in many countries and especially those with a high degree of illiteracy, population returns are at best very rough approximations. In others governments deliberately falsify the figures for political purposes. On top of this, since no one can actually count the number of births and deaths in the world, still less record their causes, the rates and their causes are largely a matter of informed guesswork. It follows that, though we can describe the scale of effects of particular famines, earthquakes and so on with a fair degree of accuracy, the provision of global statistics, and still more, global trends, is fraught with difficulty.[18]

To raise the questions about this first assumption, of course, is *not* to suppose that worries about third world poverty are baseless or that we can reasonably justify indifference to them. What matters is that realistic and effective help be given, and what prompts appeals to justice and political action, while at the same time inducing skepticism about the effectiveness of private charity, is a claim about the *scale* of the problem. But this claim, I am suggesting, is more easily made than established. If, as I suggest, the facts about world poverty are more complex than striking but simplistic slogans represent them, then scope for effective action may be much greater than the talk of 'global' trends would incline us to think. What is at stake in this issue is the degree of optimism or pessimism that is warranted.

The second assumption, that more equal distribution would alleviate distress, involves not only fact-gathering but economic theory. Considerable doubt has been cast on this claim. To begin with, the relief of material distress most obviously needs the creation of wealth, and it is highly disputable whether a more equal distribution of wealth encourages its creation. Moreover, in many places it is refugees who constitute a major problem and their difficulties arise very often not from inequality of wealth but from disruption in its creation. Refugees are generally poor, but frequently it is the very fact that they are refugees that has made them so.[19]

The third assumption, about colonial history, is more dubious still, but I shall reserve my comments upon it till the proper place in the argument. For the present, having cast a few doubts, I shall proceed on the assumption that these empirical claims are substantially *true*. This will in fact strengthen my argument for I hope to show that, even when we raise no questions about these dubious assumptions, we cannot draw from them the moral implications they are commonly thought to have.

From the first assumption it does not follow that we live in a radically unjust world. Inequality is not the same as injustice; and to suffer is not the same as to be a victim of injustice, even when the material deprivation is the same in both cases. Both these points are easy to illustrate. At the end of the football season teams are ordered according to their performance. This rarely results in equalities and never produces the result that all are equal. Now any given league table *might* be as it is because the results had been fixed or the rules bent in favor of teams with wealthy directors whose patronage needs to be encouraged for the sake of the game. In such a case the results would be unjustly arrived at and hence the final table would be unjust, but not because the positions were unequal, for we are supposing that the unequal ordering is one which *could* have been just, as it usually is. Conversely, such fixing and fudging might result in a large number of equal positionings (to accommodate equally wealthy directors, perhaps) but the result, though more equal, would be no less unjust. What the example makes evident is that justice is not the same as equality. Countless other examples will show this too. A society in which theft and fraud go on extensively but which in one year shows an equality of ill-gotten gains all round is not, for a short period, a just society. And so on.

My second point may be demonstrated no less easily. Two children are burnt to death. In one case the child dies in a forest fire started by lightning; in the second the child dies at home in a fire started by an arsonist. The material result is the same in both cases, but while in the second a great wrong has been done, in the first, though something terrible has happened, no wrong has been done. This example demonstrates that from the *fact* of suffering—pain, hunger, disease, and so on—we cannot automatically deduce that a wrong has been done. We cannot deduce, therefore, that we have good grounds for restitution or reparation or retribution.

If both these points are admitted, it follows that however incontestable the claim that there is widespread suffering in the world, this does not imply that there is widespread injustice. This is not to deny (who could?) that no decent person, to say nothing of the Christian, should be indifferent to such suffering. It is just to say that the basis of concern with it cannot be justice. This will hardly trouble those whose motivation is not a sense of justice at all but benevolent charity, for the source of their concern is *need* and this, we are assuming, is not in dispute. But those who think badly of benevolence and charity will be left with the problem of telling us why we should be bothered by world poverty at all.

One possible rejoinder is that so long as the second assumption holds good—viz., a more equal distribution would eliminate the suffering—those who prevent or fail to effect such a redistribution *are* responsible for the suffering and can legitimately be accused of acting unjustly. On this view, suffering is the product of injustice as much in the case where its relief is possible but not undertaken as it is in the case where it is deliberately brought about in the first place. Let us see whether anything of this sort really follows from our second assumption.

Suppose it is true that a radical redistribution of wealth would virtually eliminate the poverty that is crippling the inhabitants of large parts of the world. Does it follow that those rich who do not effect such a redistribution are responsible for the poverty? Common moral thinking draws a distinction between "acts" and "omissions" and holds, at a minimum, that omissions are not as morally culpable as acts—killing someone is worse than failing to save them. Of late philosophers have subjected this distinction and its moral relevance to close scrutiny and many conclude that it cannot be sustained to any purpose.[20] It seems to follow that *if* a radical redistribution of wealth would save life and prevent suffering *and* we fail to undertake it, we are, to a degree, in the same moral dock as those who cause death and injury.

There are, however, two important rejoinders to be made. From the fact, if it is one, that there is no defensible and morally relevant distinction between "acts" and "omissions" in general, it does not follow that in the particular case there is not something to be said along these lines about our behavior. If we are "killers" to the extent that we do not take those steps that will save lives, we are still different from those who, say, send poisoned food parcels to India. Further, if there is no important distinction between acting and failing to act we are entitled, presumably, to claim moral credit for *not* sending poisoned food parcels; and this merit cancels out our moral fault in failing to send nourishing ones. In short, there is here, as elsewhere, still a moral difference between those who fail to act in such a way as to relieve suffering and those who actually promote it, even if there need not be. The priest and the Levite were certainly at fault, but at least they did not cross the road and finish the job the robbers had begun.

The second point to be made here is this. The indictment of the indifferent rich rests upon the claim that "we" could radically redistribute the world's good. But who is the "we"? Plainly, the impulse to political action rests on the assumption that private individuals' enthusiasm could *not* remedy these ills, and even the heads of the wealthiest countries could not do so alone. One common error in discussion of this subject is the supposition that there is a "system" of distribution, where this way of talking is taken to imply that distribution is controlled. But it should be evident that we cannot move from the mere fact of there being a distribution to the conclusion that there is some system of distribution. There is, for example, a distribution of types of tree across the face of the earth, one that may be understood and explained, but there is no process of distributing them that we might learn to control. There is no system of tree distribution.

The same is true of wealth and of food. There is a distribution of these, but no distributor of them. We may think the distribution bad and that it should be altered, but we cannot conclude from this that there is some method of distribution which is working badly. People do think this, however. A recent Oxfam pamphlet says "There is something terribly wrong with the world food system," and goes on to invite us to play a part in "changing the system." But the metaphor of a system is misleading. It gives rise to the idea that what is being suggested is the replacement of one relatively impersonal and mechanical method with another more efficient one, whereas what the pamphlet actually calls for under the label "changing the system" are various measures that might be enacted in the policies of Western governments, trading companies, and international institutions. Changing the system turns out to be a matter of changing the decisions and behavior of those individual agents who hold public office of one sort or another. But if this is so we are back to the beginning. Individual decisions, by themselves, will not bring about a radical redistribution of the world's goods, precisely because "the system" is not under the control of individuals.

It might be replied that it is necessary for the leaders of the world to act *in concert*, and then a change of the sort desired *would* be possible. But this suggestion raises another set of problems. Let us suppose that *if* all Western governments were to give, say, 7 percent of GNP in overseas aid (i.e., ten times the recommended amount) to countries in the third world, the lives and conditions of almost all of the world's poor would be radically and irreversibly improved. Any individual politician knows very well, however, that even if he could prosecute such a policy and survive electorally in his own country, the chances are high that no other country will do the same. But if they do not, it would be folly for him to do so because not only will the desired restructuring of the world's economy *not* come about, his own country will now be at a disadvantage in comparison with its trading partners.

This is sometimes known as the problem of non-compliance. It arises with respect to any concerted action. I have an obligation, if I have, to play my part in some concerted action because of the desirability of the result of such action. But if others do not play their part that result cannot come about from my action alone, and hence I cannot have an obligation to act alone. In the case of overseas aid, the problem is very important. All we can urge any individual government to do is play its part in a concerted scheme for the sake of the end result. But recent history supplies evidence in abundance that the level of aid without strings which governments are prepared to give is falling, not rising, and consequently the grounds upon which any individual government might reject our demands are gathering strength. We should observe, of course, that this is a problem *only* where the moral basis of the demand lies in the desirability of the anticipated result of concerted action, not the anticipated result of individual action, a point of considerable importance to which I shall turn in a moment. But where the important end in view is possible *only* with the support of all, the non-compliance of some destroys the obligation on all.

This argument has a devastating effect on attempts to render world distributions just in accordance with some preconceived notion of justice. Plainly, this could only happen with the cooperation and concerted efforts of the majority of the world's richest countries. Any one of them has an obligation to play a part in bringing justice of the sort about. But none of them has an obligation to perform those actions alone. Any of them can reasonably believe that too few of the others will play their part (recent history supports this belief very well), and consequently each of them is released from the obligation. As a result no one has an obligation to do anything towards the desired result.

This is true, however, only if it is justice we are after. Aid that arises from benevolence, the demand for which rests upon *need* rather than right survives the problem of non-compliance unscathed. Or rather the inactivity of others, real or anticipated, generates no problem. If someone somewhere needs my help, and his need is a reason for me to help him, that reason remains, regardless of the fact that someone else needs someone else's help and doesn't get it. I cannot bring about social justice on my own, but I can feed some of the hungry on my own. The fact that I cannot feed them all and that others are not doing much to help does not remove my obligation to do what I can or eliminate the fact that some distress had been relieved. Here, then, is another way in which benevolence is to be preferred to "justice" as a basis of the obligation to give some overseas aid.

And there is one further advantage, along the same lines. The pursuit of justice can actually generate reasons for the *prolongation* of hunger and distress and has, in fact, not infrequently done so. If it is the case that only a few countries and individuals will give to the needy, only a proportion of the needy will be helped. Consequently, there arises a new inequality— between those who remain in abject poverty and those whose lot is in some measure improved. On some conceptions of social justice, in this way injustice is actually intensified by overseas aid. It follows, if social justice is the be-all and end-all in these matters, that we ought to resist all those programs of aid that fall short of effecting a total transformation of the condition of the poor across the face of the earth.

If my earlier argument is correct, of course, to refuse a partial remedy on the grounds that it is partial is, in the context of world poverty, to refuse all possible remedies. This throws a curious light on the propaganda of those who talk of social justice, because what they so often represent as a beacon of hope for the poor and the afflicted is in reality a counsel of despair. If the only hope is wholesale, revolutionary change, as they say, then there is no hope for the poor at all.

But even if this were not so, even if 'social justice' writ large were on the cards eventually, we should still need some reason for refusing to give or allow such help as can be given immediately. There are two familiar reasons, both of which are inadequate. First, and commonest, is the suggestion that "charity" postpones the advent of "justice." Such a view is, of course, an empirical matter and it is worth observing that, though it is often trucked out with sociological theorizing of a vaguely Marxist sort, this is largely *a priori* theorizing, that is, speculation *in advance of* examining the facts, and very rarely is any evidence actually produced in favor of the theory. My own view, for what it is worth, is that the claim is false. There seems to be some evidence for the contrary belief, that it is precisely as the lot of some section of the poor *improves* that they find a voice to make sufficient demands to secure a measure of egalitarianism. If so, charitable good works are more likely to make a greater contribution to the advent of what the protagonist of this argument calls "social justice" than not. The second argument is that charity is itself a cause of injustice and division. It is often said, for instance, that child-sponsorship schemes by providing only *some* children with food, clothing, and materials for school create a rich and poor in the classroom. But there is a grave danger here that, whatever the truth about these schemes, suffering will be tolerated, even perpetrated, out of an absurd and doctrinaire love of abstract equality.*

I have denied that justice and equality can be equated, but it does not follow that inequalities are things we do not need to be concerned about. It is clear, though, that we should certainly not be concerned about them all the time and above everything else. The confusion with justice makes this more plausible no doubt because, to some minds, justice is an overriding consideration in all human affairs. I do not myself think this, but however that may be, once we have seen that justice and equality are not the same thing, any plausibility in the view that we ought always to be concerned about equality falls away. The pursuit of *equality* for its own sake and a horror of inequalities of any kind can be shown to be absurd by some of its implications. It would, for instance, have to support the cause of nuclear war (not merely nuclear deterrence), since this would eliminate present inequalities of wealth and power far more effectively than any present schemes of redistribution

---

*The *Washington Post* for Monday, April 22, 1985, reports Nguyen Co Thach, Foreign Minister of Vietnam as saying: "Here the poverty is well distributed. Once poverty is well distributed, there is no social injustice." One doubts if the distribution is so perfect as to put the Minister on the same level as the peasants.

are likely to do. Most of us will say, of course, that we should not pursue equality at *any* price, but this is my point. Similarly, the egalitarian will have to prefer this contemporary world to one in which material inequalities are still greater, but in which the poorest are wealthy by today's standards. A world in which everyone is better off than the average middle-American of today, but in which there are individuals and countries of almost fabulous wealth will be a horrifying prospect to the enthusiastic equalizer—not, of course, to those whose concern is with hardship and suffering.

In the context of the present discussion we can agree to differ about whether or not charitable programs create troublesome inequalities (it is worth remarking that government-to-government aid, upon which proponents of "changing the system" are keenest, is that which does this most frequently),[21] and yet acknowledge that there plainly *is* a danger of being led, through misguided egalitarianism, to preferring the situation in which all the children are kept in near starvation to that in which some at least get one decent meal a day. The main point is this: we have seen no *general* grounds for deploring the necessarily piecemeal nature of charity.

I have been arguing that the bare facts of inequality and suffering do not, by themselves, imply injustice and that in any case there are serious doubts about whether the appeal to justice can provide the right sort of basis for responding to them. Let us turn now to the third assumption, one which is often supposed to acknowledge a good many of these criticisms and to go some way towards answering them. *Mere* inequality, let it now be agreed, does not imply injustice, which properly requires that the inequality has come about in certain sorts of way. Colonial history, the third assumption suggests, is one such way, namely past conquest, robbery, and subjugation. If so, we may think, in considering the relative wealth and poverty of, for instance, Europe and Africa today, that we *are* confronted with injustice.

This third assumption is the weakest of all. As P. T. Bauer has demonstrated, we have only to rehearse a few familiar facts to expose its unwarranted generality.

Whatever one thinks of colonialism, it cannot be held responsible for Third World poverty. Some of the most backward countries never were colonies, as for instance, Afghanistan, Tibet, Nepal, Liberia. Ethiopia is perhaps an even more telling example (it was an Italian colony for only six years in its long history). Again, many of the Asian and African colonies progressed very rapidly during colonial rule, much more so than the independent countries in the same area. At present one of the few remaining European colonies is Hong Kong—whose progress and prosperity should be familiar. It is plain that colonial rule has not been the cause of Third World poverty.

Nor is the prosperity of the West the result of colonialism. The most advanced and the richest countries never had colonies, including Switzerland and the Scandinavian countries; and some were colonies of others and were already very prosperous as colonies, as for instance North America and Australasia.[22]

But despite these commonly known facts, the view persists that "poverty in the Third World is a result of colonial looting in the past."[23] Suppose it *were* true. What then would follow? From the fact, when it is one, that my ancestors violated the rights of your ancestors, it does not follow that you have any claim on me. The reason is that history is composed of contingencies and we cannot engage in the history of "what might have been." For example: suppose my grandfather stole a large sum of money from your grandfather. As a result my father was able to set himself up in business and I have now inherited a considerable fortune. You, on the other hand are (relatively) poor. *If* we could say that, had my grandfather not acted in the way he did, our respective incomes would be such-and-such, there might be reason to adjust our incomes to this level by redistribution from you to me. But, of course, we cannot say this. Your grandfather, or your father, might have used the money so effectively that the position you are now denied would far exceed anything I could pay. Alternatively, your grandfather, or your father, might have squandered the money and you would have been no better off in any case. Or my father might have squandered his inheritance instead of putting it to the good use he did. And so on. Similarly in respect to the issue we are considering, granted that the facts of European colonial history are as we are assuming, nothing follows about how Europeans should act today. We could only know what to do if we knew how things would have been and this we cannot know. In the absence of such knowledge there is no contemporary injustice we can know how to remedy.[24]

Notice, too, a limitation that the importation of justice has which even the remedying of this defect could not alter. There are countries in the world that have never been the subject of European colonialism but which, because of their lack of natural resources and hostile climates, are desperately poor. If we are concerned solely with justice we will have no concern with these cases. And yet, it seems to me, insofar as there is hunger, disease, and so on, it is right to give what we can. Moreover, we should use what resources we can. The United States of America, being such a rich country, has great charitable potential, but cannot, in the name of justice, be asked to remedy past injustices in Africa and the Far East, where it has no colonial history.

I have argued that the three assumptions commonly made about suffering in the third world are largely without foundation, but that, even if they were true they would not imply any injustice on the part of the rich. I should stress, however, that such a conclusion does not carry a license to turn one's back on poverty and suffering. On the contrary. It is only those whose moral thinking is blinkered by the concepts of rights and justice who will imagine that such a conclusion follows; and indeed it is part of my objection to the contemporary obsession with justice that it has this blinkering effect. In fact my main point turns on the belief that Christians *ought* to be concerned with these facts. They *should* view as a moral demand the material as well as the spiritual needs of the destitute. But if their concern is to bring about justice, they need have *no* concern with these facts. *Ergo,* justice cannot be the basis of the Christian's concern.

(This simple argument, it seems to me, puts an end to a lot

of well-intentioned but woolly-minded talk about social justice. Because it *assumes* a legitimate concern with material suffering its conclusion that justice has next to nothing to do with
the matter cannot be accused of leading to indifference. And
precisely because it disposes of justice as a basis for Christian
concern, it opens the door once again to some other foundation. Moreover, if such a basis can be found, then since any
strictures on a Christian use of "social justice" in this connection apply equally well to secular uses of it, Christian morality
will to this extent be on firmer ground than those secular ideologies (like socialism) which, I think, Christians have often
imagined to have greater intellectual robustness.

The way is open, then, and the need revealed to find some
better basis than justice for a concern with world hunger and
the like. I think that the idea of Christian charity properly
understood does provide such a basis, but before I attempt to
show this, I want to examine one more conception of the
Christians' caring concern in politics.

III

I have argued that we cannot justifiably make religious beliefs the basis of political constitutions, and further that those
Christians who believe their political ideals may be made to
coincide with a general aspiration to a socially just society (one,
that is, which can be given a suitably secular defense) are mistaken. Lastly, I have claimed, the Christian ideal of charity,
properly understood, is in fact in a better position to provide
a moral foundation for assistance to the poor and needy than
distributive justice is. It remains to give a full account of that
ideal, and as I shall argue in the next chapter, the idea of *public*
charity is not excluded from it. This implies, contrary perhaps
to the impression created by the argument so far, that public,
even political campaigns are not necessarily excluded from the
proper concerns of the Christian and hence that the subject
of Christian politics will have to be investigated further. But

before doing so, I want to examine another line of thought which has a certain popularity at the present time. It is the belief that Christianity has, in Bishop Sheppard's phrase, a "bias to the poor." This view is not especially new. In 1909, the priest Angelo Roncalli, who was to become Pope John XXIII, was saying in the midst of a strike: "Christ's preference goes to the disinherited, the weak and the oppressed," and at many points in its history, Christians, appalled at the nakedly self-interested alliance of the church with the rich and powerful, in an effort to correct one bias, have made remarks to this effect.[25] But moreover they have felt, and it is hard to resist the feeling, that while there is something deeply *un*Christian about siding with a wealthy tyrant, there is not only nothing un-Christian but something truly Christian about siding with his victims. A church which, while professing its concern to be solely with things spiritual and ecclesiastical, nevertheless confers all the blessing of its ritual upon oppressive powers, and thus plays its part in confirming them in their self-satisfied wickedness is considerably less inspiring (and literally inspired, one is inclined to say) than one that, by those same rites, strengthens the oppressed and enables the poor to wrest some sort of dignity from their abjectness. It is this intuitive judgment, I think, which talk of "bias to the poor" means to capture. But can we draw any very concrete implications for political action from this intuition? In this third section I shall investigate this question largely by a process of clarification.

What does it mean to say that Christianity has a bias to the poor? Let us consider some possibilities. It might, at its strongest, be taken to mean that the true Christian's concern is exclusively with the poor and with their interests; that he must champion their cause in every political conflict. This strong interpretation is demonstrably false on theological grounds, I think, and highly implausible on moral grounds. In the first place it is clear, if anything is, that Christ died for all mankind, not for any one class, race, generation, or gender. There is a tendency among clergy, less marked now than formerly perhaps, to value the membership of some of their flock more than others. Just where the preference falls varies, but a good many clergy will prefer a church in which the highly intelligent and successful are members rather than the dull, talentless, and narrow-minded; or to which the politically and socially well-connected belong rather than social non-entities; or where the young (especially young men) are in much greater number than the old (especially old women). One can understand this, of course. Every clergyman must be interested in his parish's having a future and the future of a church whose members are old, poor, and without vision or talent is bleak. Nevertheless, if this understandable preference is allowed to obscure the fact that the salvation and redemption of each, no matter how old, talentless, and unattractive, is *the* first concern, a serious error has been made. Christian priests or pastors cannot rightly suppose that their mission is to one class only.

But of course the truth of this observation works every way. If it is wrong to believe that one's mission is to the rich, talented, and powerful, it is equally wrong to believe that one's mission is primarily to the poor and downtrodden. Some of Christ's recorded sayings have been allowed to mislead here, I think. Because it is said that "It is easier for a camel to go through the eye of a needle, than for a rich man to enter the Kingdom of God" some have taken this to mean that riches are an insurmountable obstacle to salvation and that consequently the rich are damned. But this is not so. When the disciples ask in astonishment, "Who then can be saved?" Jesus replies that "with God all things are possible." The rich man's way to the Kingdom is hard, no doubt, but not impossible. This is borne out by some of the Beatitudes which I quoted in the first chapter. "Blessed are the poor." Why? Because their poverty makes it easier for them to enter into the Kingdom. Now if we understand these passages straightforwardly, the implication would appear to be that the church, if it is to have a *bias* at all, should have it towards the rich since they, left to themselves, will find it very much harder to enter the Kingdom, while the poor will find it very much easier. But this conclusion needs the immediate qualification that any such mission must neither connive with nor confirm the rich in the attachment to material wealth which is the chief obstacle to their salvation.

There is an important observation to be made here. We cannot rightly suppose that the obstacle to salvation is wealth itself. To deplore the material condition of the poor is automatically to approve the remedy for it, and that remedy is wealth. Just as, and because, poverty is bad, so wealth is good. It is, as St. Paul observes to Timothy, the *love* of money that is the root of all sorts of evil. Money itself is good precisely because, properly used, it prevents suffering and degradation.[26]

Christian attitudes to wealth, in fact, have been notably ambivalent, an ambivalence that continues in the writings of many liberation theologians. On the one hand there is the belief that poverty is good, and in support of this the poverty of Christ, St. Francis, and so on is cited. On the other hand it is believed that a cardinal duty of the Christian is to work for the elimination of poverty. The only resolution of this tension lies in the view that it is poverty of *spirit* that the Christian seeks and that material poverty may, though it does not always, assist this. To this extent the materially poor are at an advantage, but they are also at some notable disadvantages. The essence of the mission to the poor is to preserve poverty of spirit while making them wealthier, and this, of course, implies a continuing Christian mission to the rich. In short, no Christian preacher, priest, or pastor could legitimately or even coherently restrict Christian mission to the poor.

A "bias to the poor," however, might be meant to carry a more social than salvationist message, conveyed in the second part of the claim we are considering—that the true Christian must champion the cause of the poor in every political conflict. But again there does not seem any good reason to accept this sort of favoritism. Can the poor do no wrong? Is it impossible that they should steal, murder, terrorize, vandalize, exploit, and destroy? The answer implied in these rhetorical questions is that the poor are as likely and maybe more likely to infringe the rights of others as any other class of persons. Indeed, it is a fairly well-established fact that the large majority of inmates in the prisons of Western democracies are from lower income groups. Of course, what implications are to be drawn from this fact is a contentious matter. Some have thought it shows that poverty causes crime, others that certain classes have a greater tendency to criminality than others. Both may be correct, in fact, but from the original truth, if it is one, that poverty causes crime it does not follow, as some vaguely suppose, that it thereby ceases to be crime. We may easily enough allow that unemployed illiterates are more likely to attack and rob defenseless old women without agreeing that their illiteracy or unemployment mitigates the evil of their actions in the smallest degree. We can also agree (whether truly or not I do not know) that anyone seriously interested in tackling crime should pursue economic policies that are likely to lead to higher employment, and still insist that those who steal, injure, and destroy before, during, or after the implementation of those policies must be caught and punished (or forced to make reparation). There is nothing inconsistent in this, which is why those who take the usual political sides on these matters generally talk past each other.

Moreover, a determination to side with the poor must to some degree be taken to imply a determination to act against others of the poor, since if it is well established that most criminals come from deprived circumstances, it is equally well established that most of the victims of crime are from these same circumstances. The point is that the expression 'bias to the poor', while no doubt intended to signify a commitment on the right side in the war against suffering and evil, cannot in fact be given this interpretation since some of the battles in that war will be against people who live in relative deprivation.

But if this is so, while our faces are set against evil and cruelty and wrong-doing wherever they may come from, and when politicians invoke the law to deal with it, we cannot declare in advance that in every political conflict our business, as Christians or as anything else, must be to side with the poor. For some at least of these will be occasions on which the relatively wealthy forces of law and order are in conflict with the relatively poor.

This last remark raises another important point of clarification. In the phrase 'bias to the poor', who is meant by 'the poor', and who, correspondingly are the rich? Bodies such as the World Health Organization sometimes offer definitions of 'the poverty line', but these are misleadingly so-called. Poverty (and wealth) is a *relative* notion twice over; if someone is said to be poor we must ask "Poor in what respect?" as well as asking "Poor in comparison to what standard?" Without answers to these questions the assertion is without meaning—like the assertion that a school is a 'great' school. Commonly, of course, answers to these questions are *assumed*—poor is taken to mean 'with respect to personal wealth, possessions, and monetary income' and comparison is made implicitly with the standard of living enjoyed by the middle classes of Europe and North America. These assumptions reflect the deep-seated materialism which dominates Western values, even among religious and moral thinkers. Material poverty is only *one* kind of poverty, as our other ways of talking confirm. "Poor health" and "poor education" are familiar and respectable expressions, which nevertheless are usually excluded from the description of poverty. (Notice how poor health is normally thought of as a result of poverty, rather than an aspect of it.) This materialistic assumption supports the idea of a Christian bias to the poor in two ways. First, it leads us to suppose, falsely, that there is a definable class "the poor," and to suppose that they, being the poor, have first claim to our attention. But the materially rich can have a poor education, enjoy only poor health, live emotionally or spiritually poor lives, while the existence of Abraham Lincolns and Mother Theresas reminds us that learning, influence, wisdom, and fame are not always beyond the reach of those who have little or even no money. It follows that when we are told that a Christian must have a bias to the poor, we must ask "Poor in what?"

In response to this sort of point it is sometimes suggested that these other aspects of poverty are secondary, that material poverty is the most important. But this response reflects the same materialistic prejudice to which Western thought is prey. Belief in the superior value of material riches is far from universal and we must not suppose that those who are very poor by Western standards consider themselves to lead near worthless lives.[27] Indeed, if we take suicide to be an indication on the part of those who kill themselves that life is not worth living, there is evidence to the contrary, for suicide rates in the third world are very much lower than those in the rich countries of the West.

This, in fact, is one part of the second relativity we should remember, "Poor by what standard?" Poverty is relative to available riches. The "poor" in Britain today can usually afford a sufficiency of food (if not of a very high or varied standard) and some measure of sophisticated entertainment (a television, usually). For the most part they have tolerable housing, a large measure of protection against ill-health, their children are being educated and can look forward to a better future, in many cases with good reason. Now this is certainly a limited life, and not one that most people living in the Western world at the present time would envy, but it is only relative to such people that it can be called "poverty." For the vast majority of people who lived before 1910 or so, this existence *would* have been enviable, having as it does a much higher degree of protection against the evils of this world—hunger, ill-health, ignorance—than they could ever reasonably have hoped for. And in comparison to the majority of the *world's* inhabitants at the present time the lot of the Western "poor" is also very desirable for the same reasons as it would have appealed to earlier ages and because, for most peasants, to be able to survive in unemployment would be to be free of unremitting toil.

Of the bias to the poor, then, we must ask "To whom is it a bias?" Ought we to ignore the poorest in British society on the grounds that they are rich in comparison to those far away? The question is complicated further by the first relativity I mentioned. Since a poor family might be a healthier, happier family than many whose incomes are much higher, should our bias be to those who are in material or emotional poverty?

There is no answer to these questions it seems to me, and in fact we do not need any. The whole conception of "the poor" as a social or political class is misguided. "The poor" is that class which is in *need* of one kind or another, a class to which we properly all belong as far as redemption and salvation are concerned, and probably all belong from time to time as far as emotional needs are concerned. On this reading, the claim that Christians have a bias to the poor is *axiomatically* true. Insofar as they ought to be moved by charity they will regard the needs of others as a reason for action. But it will not carry the implication that they are specially devoted to the service of one class, any more than it will carry the implication that they are the servants of one race, even though a given race may at one time and as a matter of contingent fact stand in much greater need than any other race (as blacks did in the Southern states of America).

It follows that talk of a "bias to the poor," if it is not the axiom I have suggested it is, is either a confusion or a mere rhetorical device for expressing the good intentions of some, while at the same time allowing them to avoid specificity in their proposals. The claim that the Christian church should always take the part of the poorer party in political conflicts cannot, as a general doctrine, commend itself, and only appears to do so when it is allied with a social and political theory of a more or less Marxist stripe, an alliance I discuss in an appendix. The reason is that such a recommendation invites us to be *prejudiced*, to decide who is right and who is wrong *before* looking into the matter. This is not a policy (*pace* some Burkeian conservatives) that can ever be rationally justified by those who believe that there is truth in these matters, as I argued in chapter one the Christian must do. Nor do I think that most of those who have spoken of a bias to the poor have meant to endorse this uncompromising doctrine. But what they do not see, perhaps, is that there is no other version of the bias which does not lose the specificity of this interpretation — either our political allegiance is made clear in this implausible fashion or else the implausibility is removed at the cost of making our political allegiance *un*clear.

It might be said that I have myself made use of the notion of "need" which is also a relative notion (apart perhaps from some very basic needs for minimal amounts of food and water). It can hardly be in any better position than "poverty" therefore. But this objection would be a good one only if I had tried to offer a *substantial* substitute interpretation of the bias. In fact what I offered was an interpretation which showed it to be a theoretical axiom of Christian charity, not a practical recommendation. To say, as I do, that it is a fundamental feature of charity that the needs of others will constitute a reason for action (which is not, it seems to me, a feature of justice) is not to say where these needs will be found or what sorts of needs they are. The popular conception of a Christian bias to the poor, on the other hand, does carry and is meant to carry, I think, the implication that there is one specifiable set or class of persons to whose needs the Christian should be oriented. The relativity of "the poor," I claim, makes this substantial interpretation either objectionable or meaningless.

Once we have seen this we will see, I think, that the expression of love of neighbor cannot take a peculiarly political expression. Most Latin American liberation theologians, it should be noted, do not subscribe to this general doctrine anyway. They claim only to speak and write within the context and experience of contemporary South America. To this degree my conclusion does not directly challenge much of what they have to say, but only the generality that others have lent it, a generality, nevertheless, on to which liberation theology, I am inclined to think, will always be driven.

In these last two chapters I have been concerned to reveal what I take to be the inadequacies of two familiar conceptions of Christian charity and of its implications in the modern world. My criticisms of them have been of two sorts. First, they ally

Christian charity with other, more secular, conceptions (of counseling and justice, respectively) to which there are moral and other intellectual objections. Second, and perhaps more importantly, they do this in an effort to win credence, while in that very effort removing the Christian character of charity. Such arguments as I have brought, however, will remain forever negative if we cannot give a more successful account of Christian charity. Indeed, in the absence of such an account, the second sort of criticism is quite without weight, because if there is *no* account of Christian charity to be had—no clear conception which while retaining the character of charity finds a solid basis in the ethics of repentance—it is hardly an objection to other accounts that they fail to realize it. Conversely, if there *is* such a positive account, the first sort of criticism is strengthened by it. If we can find a distinctively Christian charity which is *not* subject to the moral objections which may be brought against secular alternatives (roughly, manipulation in the case of counseling, indifference in the case of justice) that conception will have much to recommend it, *independently* of its being Christian. And that, as I suggested briefly in chapter one, might in fact provide a basis for Christian belief. Everything turns, then, on a positive account of true Christian charity. This is the subject of the fourth and final chapter.

CHAPTER FOUR

CHARITY AND REPENTANCE

What is true Christian charity, and what makes it truly Christian? I have suggested that we can arrive at a satisfactory answer to this question only if we locate charity in what I earlier called the <u>ethics of repentance</u>, something which I believe can indeed be done, provided we are clear just what repentance is. But before saying more on this point I should like to consider two familiar, though to my mind inadequate, ideas of the connection between Christian belief and conduct.

In his book *The Virtues*[1] Peter Geach argues vigorously that the virtue of charity is love of God, not love of man, and that many of the things that pass for charity—like giving to the poor—have nothing to do with the real virtue. Now while it may be correct to say that at the heart of true charity is love of God, there is plainly a component in the virtue which consists in compassionate concern for other people, and this requires us to consider what the relation between these two aspects might be. For the moment I shall be concerned with charity as love of fellow human beings, and will return to love of God towards the end of this chapter.

I

It is sometimes said that the obligation of charity arises from the brotherhood of all people, which in its turn arises from the fatherhood of God. "The brotherhood of all," of course, is not a distinctively Christian conception and may be found in the writings of many of the more Utopian socialists and anarchists. Indeed, it is reasonable to dispute the suggestion that it is a *Christian* conception at all, since in the Johannine literature of the New Testament where something of the sort makes a frequent appearance, the terms 'brother' and 'brethren' are used exclusively to refer to the early Christians themselves, *not* the whole of humanity;[2] and, when Jesus wished to draw attention to moral relationships which hold across conventional boundaries, between Jews and Samaritans for instance, he talked of neighborliness rather than brotherhood. But even if we grant that the brotherhood of all follows from the fatherhood of God and hence *is* a Christian conception, we are no nearer making charity an important Christian virtue. Let us suppose, though it could reasonably be doubted, that something about the *natural* relationships of brotherhood and sisterhood does imply that siblings ought to have compassionate concern for the needs of each other. The argument that gets us from this to universal charity is, presumably,

> Brothers and sisters ought to care for each other
> All human beings are brothers and sisters
> *Therefore*
> We ought all to care for each other.

But such an argument, though it appears valid, rests upon an ambiguity in the term 'brother and sister'. In a perfectly obvious and straightforward sense we are *not* all related to each other as brothers and sisters, so that the sense of brotherhood (if any) in which all humankind *are* brothers cannot be quite the same as the sense in which they are not. But without the assumption that the "brotherhood" which follows from the fatherhood of God carries the same moral implications as natural brotherhood, the argument is invalid. Further, since it is quite implausible to think that the moral implications could be *all* the same (*prima facie* one ought to attend one's brother's wedding or funeral, but not everyone's) the argument just given *is* invalid. In other words, even if we agree (which we do not) that the brotherhood of all is a Christian conception, and that charity begins at home (i.e., one ought to be charitable to members of one's own family), this does not imply that one ought to be charitable to all humankind.

An alternative, equally familiar but somewhat simpler line of thought is this: Christ reveals that God cares for us and for all that He has made. In return for His love for us, we should love those things He loves. As I remarked in the first chapter, though there would appear to be something right in this way of thinking, there is also something less than perspicuous about it. If God loves us we should love Him, let us suppose, but it follows that we should love those whom He loves only if we grant a principle of transitivity which seems implausible, namely

If X cares about Y, and if X cares about Z
Then
If Y ought to care about X, Y ought to care about Z.

But is this any more plausible than saying: If Joe invites Bill to dinner (so that Bill should invite Joe back), then if Joe invites Sam to dinner, Bill should invite Sam to dinner.

The analogy, it might be said, is misleading. The principle of transitivity is restricted to attitudes of caring – if I care about someone shouldn't I care about the things that matter to them. 'Yes' is the answer, but only because the other cares about them, and not for their own sake. It is a limited sort of caring. For instance, if my wife loves a dog I could well do without, I will no doubt take care of the dog for her sake. But not for *its* sake. In this sense, I do not care for it at all. Love, then, enters into the explanation of my actions towards the dog but it is not love *for the dog*.

Similarly, if I care for others only because they matter to God, I am not, strictly speaking, caring for *them* at all. This is one objection that might be raised to the parable of the judgment in Matthew 28. The way Jesus is recorded as telling the story suggests that it is only because in attending to the needs of the hungry, the thirsty, strangers, and those in prison, we are caring and failing to care for God, that these are significant facts when it comes to the last judgment; that the needs of the hungry, thirsty, and so on are not important *in themselves*, but only as a means to pleasing God. This is not the only possible interpretation, but it illustrates the necessity, if we are to lend Christian charity a good name, of preserving the centrality of the needs of those towards whom we act. Both these points may be illustrated by analogy. If I love my children, someone may hurt and displease me by ridiculing them. They may hurt and displease me in other ways too, of course. Now if they do ridicule my children, it is open to me to say that other blandishments are worthless because in treating my children in this way they undo any effect these other blandishments might have had. But it nevertheless remains true that what I am concerned about is my children's being ridiculed, not my displeasure, and can distinguish between those who have no inclination to ridicule my children, and hence are pleasant company for me, and those who would do so though they do not out of fear of my displeasure.

The point is, the story in Matthew can be interpreted in this way; our interest in the needy should coincide with God's. This need not be taken to mean that caring for others is only important as a means to pleasing God. But the general injunction we are considering—care about others because God cares for them—does have this implication as it stands and must leave the needs of others out of the picture. It thus leaves it unclear whether our attitude can be called care for *them* at all.

I have said that charity must be found a home in the ethics of repentance. To my mind only such a context will provide a convincing explanation of the Christian character of this virtue. But if my arguments against these last two lines of thought are sound, such a context may provide the only basis for the virtue of charity that there is. An account of Christian charity which locates it in the ethics of repentance will thus have the double virtue of uniting the moral and religious in the

New Testament and of being, perhaps, the only explanation of charity there is.

Repentance is often thought of as the attitude of being sorry for what one has done. No doubt as the word is often used this is the proper understanding, and indeed it might be said that *any* notion of repentance must include some such element of specific repenting for past deeds. But as the Greek *metanoia* suggests, in Christian theology we must give the term a rather larger connotation so that it captures the idea of a change of heart consequent upon a change of understanding. This expression of a changed understanding is what is often referred to as "seeing the light," that is, perceiving the truth. And this truth is that God is the ruler of all things and that the essential characteristic of His rule is love for His creation. To be a Christian is to acknowledge this truth as revealed in Jesus, "not only with our lips, but in our lives." That is to say, the truth we acknowledge is a practical truth — like the truth that strychnine is poisonous — not merely a theoretical one, for God's rule is, so to speak, twofold. First, He is that power which actually controls all things — nature, men, angels, devils, — and second, He is the source of anything that we can regard as right or good. In the Kingdom of God, then, fact and value come together — the world is as it is because it is good, and good is what it is because God has created as He has and will bring to fulfillment as He will. Thus it is wrong to think of our moral sensibilities independently of God's creative activity. Pain and suffering are evil for what they are, and they are what they are because God has made them so. Similarly, human love and human pleasure are good because of what they are, and they are what they are because God has made human beings what they are. To acknowledge God's goodness, then, leaves no place whatever for striking out on our own. There is no *rational* alternative, if the Christian God does rule, but to obey Him. Anything else is perverse and foolish.

The Christian must not only agree but assert, however, that the Kingdom of God is at present incomplete. By God's own command human beings (and devils and angels if there are such) are free to reject His rule, and even to work against it (as we may suppose Satan to do). Only ignorance, stupidity, or sheer willfulness can explain the fact that there are men and women who do not "reck His rod," for there can at most be only temporary success for even the best laid schemes which are not in accordance with His will. Furthermore, and this is a point of some importance, the success of human schemes must always be somewhat deceptive. Since God is ultimately in charge, even their temporary success depends upon His grace, His forbearance, that is to say, in allowing them to happen. As Peter Geach remarks

> Nebuchadnezzar had it forced on his attention that only by God's favour did his wits hold together from one end of a blasphemous sentence to another—and so he saw that there was nothing for him but to bless and glorify the King of Heaven, who is able to abase those who walk in pride.[3]

Just *why* God allows some of these temporary successes (Nazi concentration camps, communist purges, and so on) is the subject matter of the 'problem of evil', but that is not our problem here. It is enough to observe, for present purposes, that if God is the maker and judge of all things, then it is a fact that they persist only because He allows them.

If all this is true, what conclusions follow for human conduct? Men and women are free beings. We may choose to live as we wish, within certain limits. The fact that reason suggests the wisdom of this course rather than another does not compel us to follow its suggestions. But if we *are* to live wisely and well, given the revelation of God in Christ, we cannot do better than to conjoin our wills with God's, to make them one with His, and to abandon those causes and courses by which, deliberately or in ignorance, we set our wills against His. Communion, atonement, is the only reasonable hope. We shall have located the distinctively Christian virtues if we can pinpoint those that follow from this hope. I shall argue that charity is one such virtue, but to show this plainly it is necessary to return to some of the topics of previous chapters.

II

It is foolishness to set oneself against God, but equally foolish to set oneself to do without God. This dependence upon God, however, appears to be at odds with an ethical ideal upon which I have relied in my criticism of both psychological healing and the idea of a Christian society, namely autonomy or the self-determination of the individual. What needs to be shown is that subscription to this ideal is compatible with a belief in the Christian revelation, and that an attitude of repentance is possible in those who regard themselves as self-determined.

Individualism is an ideal that has met with more criticism than endorsement in the last fifty years, though it is worth emphasizing my earlier remark that socialists who have rejected it have done so only because of their belief in the inefficiency of the model of society that customarily accompanies it. At bottom they *share* the ideal since it is for the flourishing of the individual that the revolutionary restructuring of society is usually said to be needed. Just what the ideal *is*, however, is not always clear. There are at least two ways of conceiving it. One we might call social or political, a belief that social arrangements should leave the individuals as free as possible to determine their activities for themselves, the other a more substantive moral or personal ideal, sometimes called "possessive individualism" according to which individuals should aim to be beholden to no one and to claim, consequently, all and only that which is theirs by right. This will usually be the mode of existence which they have chosen through their own designing intelligence and those things they have come to possess by the sweat of their brow, the free gift of another, or through contractual arrangements voluntarily entered into. In the light of this ideal the honest self-made man is king and all limitations placed upon him in the form of taxes, established religion, compulsory education and so on, are *prima facie* evils which can only be justified insofar as they can be shown to be necessary for the promotion of possessive individualism itself.

As this last sentence suggests, the ideal of possessive individualism is usually thought to imply a radical political philosophy of a liberal sort, often known as libertarianism, and for this reason a rejection of the ideal is frequently taken to imply a rejection of political liberalism. But of course the reasoning behind such a belief is invalid, an instance of what is known to logicians as 'denying the antecedent,' in fact. We can separate the social philosophy from the moral ideal and may well find reasons to accept the first while rejecting the second. Indeed my purpose in this chapter is to do just that and to show that Christian theology provides reason to accept liberal individualism while rejecting the ideal of the self-made man.

Since individual human beings as we find them just *are* free, in the sense that they are capable of and have a natural tendency to pursue self-chosen goals, the only alternative to a liberal individualistic society is a corporatist one, that is, a society ordered according to a strict hierarchy in which individuals are given a station, where they take all and only those decisions which, so to speak, come with that station, and where the society as a whole is ordered from the top.

I shall say something shortly about what is objectionable in such a society, but first I need to defend the contentious assertion that corporatism is the only alternative to a liberal individualistic society. Many have argued, among them many Christians, that there is a third possibility — a cooperative society in which individuals freely cooperate for the common good rather than compete in the pursuit of individual goods. Now the cooperative society has certain obvious attractions but as an ideal it is inherently unstable, that is to say, it contains the seeds of its own destruction. This is because it rests upon the *contingency* of cooperation. It is logically impossible to guarantee the outcome of any free exercise of the will.[4] Structure the cooperative society as you will, therefore, given that it is an association of *freely* cooperating individuals, there is always the possibility that they freely cease to cooperate. At this point in their association, the pursuit of the common good can be relegated to the realm of personal choice or abandoned altogether, or it can be maintained by compulsion and coercion on the part of the state—hence my claim that a corporate state is the only real alternative to a free association of individuals. For the *compulsory* cooperative state (if not a contradiction in terms) is objectionable in precisely the same way as the corporate state—it unwarrantedly assumes the inequality of different members of society, the rulers and the ruled. If a cooperative enterprise is maintained through compulsion, there is a clash of wills, the will of those who would withdraw from the enterprise and the will of those who want its continuation (the sort of clash dramatically illustrated by the East German exodus of 1989). The use of compulsion, if it is to be rationally defensible, must assume that the will of the second is superior in foresight, understanding, benevolence, or in some other way. And this carries the implication, of course, that the will of the first is inferior, a denial, in short, of its equality. So, those who use compulsion to continue collective farming against the will of the peasants who would prefer to farm their own plots of ground must assume that they have greater knowledge, or justice or benevolence behind their actions than the peasants can have behind theirs, if they are not to be guilty of a quite arbitrary exercise of power.

Of course, this conclusion does not amount to a refutation of the claims of the corporate state. Arguments have been advanced from the time of Plato to support the contention that we should not regard the free decision of every adult as equally important. First, it might be said, some people just *are* more enlightened, better informed, better intentioned than others, and second, there is no reason to think that one individual's will should prevail over that of the majority. The first observation, however, though true, is not to the point. To begin with the corporatist must show that it is possible to *institutionalize* the superior will, to ensure that it is always the more enlightened who exercise greater power, because it is not at all evident that more intelligent or better intentioned people generally come to the top in corporatist societies like Fascist Italy or the Soviet Union. But in any case, the context we are considering is one in which there is a clash between the individual who would pursue some goal, not necessarily a selfish one, and the continuance of a cooperative enterprise. We cannot say in *advance of* any particular circumstances that the will of those who would compel cooperation is superior to the will of those who would go their own way without at the same time presupposing the superior value of the cooperative enterprise, which is precisely what is under dispute. Similarly, of course, we cannot assume the superiority of the individual's project, but this is not a danger in the case in question since he or she does not seek to compel others to refrain from cooperation. Peasant farmers rarely if ever seek the right to make others leave the collective, only the right to leave it themselves.

This might be disputed. We know of many instances, it will be said, when an individual's refusal to cooperate wrecks the agreed plans of a large number of others. In such circumstances, to favor the recalcitrant individual *is* to assume that the rights of an individual are more important than the common goal of everyone else.

That such conflicts arise cannot be denied, and it is implausible to maintain that they must always be settled in favor of the individual. Such things as compulsory purchase orders which, in my view, ought to be set around with many safeguards and used sparingly, can nevertheless be justified. But they cannot be justified on the ground that the common good is more important than individual freedom without begging the question at issue, namely whether we should favor the projects of a cooperative society. If they are to be justified it is as a consequence of the will of the majority. This brings us to the second point mentioned above.

The view that the will of the majority ought to prevail over that of the individual might be expanded in two different ways. On one interpretation the will of the majority is *superior*. But why should we think this? If one person can be wrong, why cannot a number of persons? And why not, therefore, the majority? On a second interpretation, the will of the majority ought to prevail, not because it is superior, but just because it is the majority's. To this interpretation we need have no objection, but this is because some mechanism for the resolution of conflicts is needed in any society, and majority voting, within limits, seems better than most. It is better to count heads than to break them. But this means that on the second interpretation of the value of democracy, institutional arrangements through which the will of the majority is expressed are to be valued only as useful political devices for the peaceful resolution of conflicts of interest and opinion, not as the 'voice of the people' which transcends the limited aspirations and altruism of self-seeking individuals. In short, on the acceptable version of the importance of democracy, we have no reason to think of the general will as any more than the confluence of the wills of the majority of self-directed individuals.

It follows that the cooperative ideal is inherently unstable and persists only so long as the individuals in a free society choose to make it persist, and can win permanence only by being converted into a corporate state in which each is *given* rather than chooses his place in the society's enterprises. Faced with *this* choice, that is, faced with the impossibility of freely perpetuated cooperation, the vast majority, I submit, will choose an individualist society, except, usually, those who expect to be in charge in the corporate state.

I should perhaps stress the difference between my argument and one that is first found most plainly stated in the writings of David Hume. According to Hume a society of freely cooperating individuals would be possible if human beings were less selfish. But the fact is that they *are* selfish and this (in consideration with other facts often referred to as the "conditions of justice") makes liberal justice the only viable form of social organization. My argument however (which is not novel) does not rely on the supposition that sooner or later individuals will want to withdraw from the cooperative enterprise for *selfish* reasons, but only that they will want to withdraw for reasons of some sort (including highly principled reasons). Though it may be true that human beings are incurably selfish, it is also true that they have conflicting opinions on what things are good and bad, and it is this second feature, at least as much as the first, and probably more importantly, that makes the cooperative society unstable.[5] The corresponding defect in corporatism, therefore, is an assumption on the part of its rulers that they are better able to judge what is good than those they rule, and it is the assumption of superiority in *this* respect which, I shall argue, is objectionable.[6]

It is for the reasons just outlined that we are obliged to prefer a liberal individualistic society. But this fundamental preference does not in its turn require us to accept the politics of libertarianism, to be champions of the free market and the right to carry arms, for instance. It does not even oblige us to accept the ideals of anarcho-liberalism, for there are different strands of this ideal which may be distinguished and need not all imply each other. I propose now to distinguish three different facets of the ideal of the autonomous individual, to show how acceptance of the first of these reinforces the rejection of corporatism, and to discuss the compatibility of these three features with the fundamental conceptions of Christianity that I have been exploring. I shall argue that of the three—basic equality, personal independence, and self-reliance—only the first two are values the Christian should accept. And the reasons to reject the third are those which can be made to show the place and importance of Christian charity.

III

Kantian liberal morality of the kind to which I have referred insists upon the fundamental equality of human beings. This belief needs to be stated carefully, because rather obviously there are a great many respects in which adult human beings are *not* equal. Some have been tempted to construe the belief in a prescriptive rather than descriptive way, to construe it; that is to say, as the expression of a resolution to treat human beings equally rather than a description of the human condition. But this approach is not altogether satisfactory since it so easily leaves the assertion of equality without any basis. Why should we respect, still less share someone's resolve to treat human beings equally rather than someone else's resolve to treat them unequally, especially in view of the fact that there are clear differences between people? The best foundation for *not* treating children on a par with adults, for instance, would seem to lie with the fact that they are in reality importantly different. So there is reason to interpret the belief in the equality of all human beings *descriptively* in order then to justify and explain equality of treatment. Remembering, however, the differences that do exist in skill, intelligence, beauty, character, and so on, it is equally important to be very clear about the respect in which adult human beings *are* equal and the relative importance of this feature in their lives and the organization of their societies. The belief in equality, therefore, must run something like this: whereas *all* normal adult human beings are superior in understanding and accomplishment to all young children, whose understanding is inadequate to the task of pursuing their own interests, sufficient to justify the paternalistic institutions of family, school, and so on, *no* individual adult or group of adults is *so* superior, and none so inferior, to warrant institutions for the paternalistic ordering of human affairs. In short, just as it is a fact that all are born weak and helpless, so it is a fact that the vast majority grow up to a roughly similar level of maturity. Of course there are exceptions—child prodigies, geniuses, world-class athletes, as well as the mentally retarded and the insane. But the restricted nature of the attributes in which such great differences are possible—music, chess, math, and the like—and the very small number of those who are very seriously incapacitated make these clearly exceptional. There is no reason to think that great athletic or intellectual ability makes for practical wisdom or moral sensitivity, and no more reason to extend the special treatment which the mentally feeble need to the whole of society, than there is to organize universities on the assumption that all students will be geniuses. This is not to deny, certainly, that there *are* differences in the prudence, benevolence, ignorance, and imagination of individuals, only to deny that such differences are either great enough or firmly enough rooted in the life of the individual or in any one social group to lend a rational basis to their institutionalized dominion or subjugation. The most intelligent individual can suffer senile decay, the ablest politician can be subject to other weaknesses (as Pitt the Younger was to drink), the stupidest parents can give birth to brilliant children, the most feckless to entrepreneurs. These are facts, and the assertion of the equality of all is at its strongest when it is based upon these facts, and whatever one's social or individual purposes, it will be wise to accommodate them. It will be wise, in short, to be an egalitarian in this sense.

These facts tell most strongly against all forms of corporatism, be they Fascist or communist. Plato could think otherwise because his theory of moral knowledge both offered an explanation of the general fallibility of mankind and made possible the emergence of an infallible philosopher-king. Without that theory, which we now know to be inadequate, there is no ground for his belief, but in order to reject corporatism we need not deny that in theory there *could* be ideal rulers; we need only deny that there *are*, or are likely to be any. This is enough to show some form of egalitarianism to be inescapable.

The claims that we might make for an ideal ruler, then, cannot reasonably be made for any actual ruler, but they are not any more defensible when they are made on behalf of "the people" as a whole. The proper reflection of the recognition of basic human equality is not the ideal of democracy but the belief in 'checks and balances', that is, in constitutional arrangements which put limits on the power that may be exercised, even when those in office enjoy the support of a large majority of present voters.

A defense of the liberal social order, then, depends upon the claim of human equality. This is the point at which we can see the consonance of liberalism with Christian theology, for if the Christian revelation is true there is another dimension on which human beings are fundamentally equal—in their need for salvation. According to the Kerygma everyone needs to recognize the Kingdom of God as revealed in Christ and no one has, so to speak, a head start in this matter. Since there can be no more essential or fundamental orientation to the world than the individual's relationship to God, it follows that the equality of all people is a fundamental truth about them. Christian theology, therefore, has its own account of the basic equality of human beings which, at a minimum is quite compatible with the sort of natural equality which lies at the heart of individualism, and at a deeper level, where we stress the creative activity of God, explains that natural equality.

Someone might contest the idea that no one has a head start in the business of salvation. Surely, it will be said, those who live in a Christian country and have had a Christian upbringing are much more likely to be able to acknowledge the Kingdom of God than those who live in atheistic or heathen countries? And this increased probability just *is* a head start. Rather obviously large issues with a long history are raised here, but it will have to suffice to say that, if we could conceive of obedience to God as a skill which might result from training, then the idea that a Christian education advances an individual's salvation would have some plausibility. The truth is, however, that obedience to God is a more complex matter than this. It is possible for the whole apparatus of institutionalized religion, even for religious attitudes themselves, to contrive estrangement from God, to become corruptions of true religion.[7] This probability implies that the chances of religious error (usually in the form of pride) is also increased in a Christian country, and, given the cancelling out of probabilities, this means that a fundamental equality is restored. Two other objections need to be considered, however.

It might be supposed, and has been supposed by some Christians, that Christian theology implies an *in*equality, namely that between the saved and the damned, the elect and the rest. This idea, of course, raises some of the most fundamental and perennial questions of Christian theology, which I cannot hope to deal with adequately here. A few reasons can be given, however, for thinking that any human discrimination between the saved and the damned is bound to be untrustworthy and is, therefore, one which we can have no good reason to institutionalize.

There are a number of general and interrelated strands of thought on the subject of the things necessary for salvation. The theory of predestination, as is well known, derives the certainty of the salvation of the elect, regardless of their conduct in this life, and the equal certainty of the damnation of those who are not among the elect, from the omnipotence and omniscience of God. On such a view human beings are not fundamentally equal since some are among God's elect and others are most decidedly not. But even if true, this doctrine would give the Christian believer no reason to make any discriminations in this life. First, it is not at all evident how the elect are to be identified (though notably fervent Calvinists, without much reason, believed themselves rather than others to be among the elect) and second the doctrine itself implies that there can be no reason to act one way rather than another with respect to moral or social questions, since what one does and what happens has no bearing whatever on the eventual fate of the individual or of the society. The sorts of laws passed in Scotland under the inspiration of the Duke of Argyll in the reign of Charles II,[8] for instance, are quite without foundation in Calvinist theology. So, too, was the individual's voluntary abstinence from pleasurable activities.

In a quite different way Roman Catholic theology has tried to place the keys of heaven and hell, as it were, in the hands of a specific class of persons—the prelates—by making the church, through the sacraments and other media, the sole possessor of the means of salvation. The theology of the sacraments is, of course, a very complex area, but I am inclined to assert that any account of the sacraments that attempts to remove from God the final judgment of the individual or attempts to manipulate divine grace as though it were an implement for the achievement of human purposes is on the one hand an expression of gross *hubris* (as well as the utmost foolishness) and on the second a degeneration from sacrament to magic.

These are contentious assertions and could only be substantiated by a sustained examination of the theologies involved, and in the absence of this we need some other way of driving a wedge between the theology and the moral and social views which it may be thought to imply. But such a wedge is to be found, in fact, in the argument I used earlier against the idea of a Christian society. Let it be the case that the true church, through the sacraments instituted by God in Christ, is possessed of the power of salvation and damnation. We are left with the question: which is the true church? for there are more claimants than one. Plainly, there is no reason to accept the assertion of any one church that *it* is the true church, since part of the mark of corruption is certain to be the conviction with which the false Christs assert their authenticity. It may be replied that from the fact that there are more claimants than one, it does not follow that all of them have equally good claims. Indeed it might be the case that there are many claimants but only one which can in fact summon a sufficiently substantial historical link to sustain its claim with any plausibility. It must be agreed, I think, that this is a possibility and that agnosticism about which is the true church is not legitimized merely by the existence of different claimants. But notoriously we cannot reason from what could be to what is, and must recognize it as a fact that more churches than one have plausible grounds upon which to claim lineage from Apostolic Christianity. Given further that there are important differences in the views of these churches on the conduct proper to a Christian, it follows that we have no reason to implement any of this 'theology of the true church' into social arrangements in the form of inquisitions, ecclesiastical courts, and the like, and no reason to adopt uncritically the prelates of one church as moral authorities.

A third and final strand of thought is to be found in certain branches of evangelical Protestantism. Here the idea is that, though all men *initially* need salvation, anyone can, simply by accepting Christ, be assured of salvation. Those who deny this, it will be said, deny an essential aspect of the Kerygma—its promise of the assurance of salvation. Consequently, we can assert that there are those who are saved and those who are not, so that all men are not equal. But though this view rightly draws our attention to the dynamic of salvation (something which the doctrine of predestination denies) it does not give the full dynamic. If men and women can be saved, they can also backslide, if they can be penitent they can also come to harden their hearts. To turn the saved into the elect this theology needs to make an assumption of permanence which is unrealistic. The permanence of the elect in Calvinist theology derives from the nature of God. It is precisely because, in this view, the individual has no part to play in his or her own salvation that the vicissitudes of human behavior do not affect the issue. But where the individual's turning to God is made an essential part of salvation, the possibility of his turning away again cannot be discounted. If this is so we have, once more, no reason to institutionalize the differences between those who are Christians and others, and no reason, therefore, to amend the earlier contention that Christian theology explains and endorses what I have called the natural equality of all men.

The arguments I have used to this conclusion have attempted to sidestep the theological issues involved. This is a useful strategy since those issues are so intractable. But I should like to record my view that there is a deep compatibility between the belief in the basic equality of human beings and the picture of Christ in the Gospels. Pretty consistently they present Him as one who does not make any fundamental distinction between prostitutes, publicans, decent ordinary Jews, members of the occupying Roman forces, hated Samaritans, tax-gatherers, lepers, children, rabbis, and madmen. And several of the parables, notably that of the two men in the temple, convey a strong sense of the importance of true humility. For these reasons, I would contend, any institutional arrangement or social custom which divides human beings systematically into superior and inferior classes or races or nationalities or genders is deeply unChristian.

I conclude that liberal moral theory and Christian theology converge on the assertion of the basic equality of all men and women. No race, gender, class, or other group is naturally or permanently better, more entitled to respect or authority than any other. This is not because all are equally precious or equally clever or good, but because, with the exceptions I noted earlier, all are equally subject and susceptible to foolishness, petty-mindedness, spite, cruelty, selfishness, insensitivity, and so on, and all are capable to much the same degree of affection, hope, charity, nobility, faith, and of responding to divine grace. It follows from neither liberal morality nor Christian theology, however, that all should be treated alike, or that the goods of this world should be regarded as common property to be shared out equally or that the means of production should be held in common (which in practice means held by the state and controlled by its officers). To treat slow learners as though they were quick is no kindness to them, and to overlook or ignore important differences on the grounds that to do otherwise is discriminatory is plain foolishness, two lessons which some of the more doctrinaire proponents of anti-discrimination campaigns would do well to learn. Liberal morality has stressed the importance of respecting the rights of others, that is, acknowledging their rights as equal to our own, and Christian morality must emphasize the equal importance of needs—that our needs are no more important than the needs of others. It may be that it is at this point that the two diverge again, a suggestion I shall not explore here, but in any event we have seen reason enough to conclude that at a more fundamental level they are agreed. Just what the belief in basic equality implies in the way of attitudes and institutions, I shall not now discuss.

IV

The second feature of liberal morality to be examined is the independence or separateness of persons. This shows itself most plainly, and is grasped most readily perhaps, in the idea of a right to privacy. There are things that we can do to other people which are not harmful and may even be beneficial which, nevertheless, the idea of respect for the autonomy of persons rules out. This is not because it values self-direction, something I shall discuss in the next section, but because it attributes to the individual a right to a certain sphere of privacy. So, for instance, listening in to the telephone conversations of others, even if it does no harm and might do good by enabling the listener to advise the callers of more profitable contracts, for instance, is still something which common moral thinking rules out. Likewise, the forcible introduction of communal living of the sort Plato envisaged might indeed improve the economic and political condition of a society very greatly, but it involves depriving the individual of something which this greater good does not, from the point of view of liberal individualism, justify. Again, to construe the value of education solely in terms of its social benefits—the provision of the doctors, engineers, and so on that "society" needs—and to ignore its value for the individual who is educated is to make a deep mistake.

This last example, in fact, shows that the mistake is not merely a mistake from the liberal point of view, but an evaluation that everyone who accepts the basic equality of human beings must acknowledge as mistaken. If someone were to ask why we should value the institutions that produce good doctors, the answer must be that health is valuable. Health, however, is not an abstract commodity, but a property of individuals. Consequently the root idea is the value that attaches to healthy individuals, something which those individuals will themselves value, but something which we must value too, if we value the production of "useful" people like doctors. Someone might resist this conclusion by insisting that healthy individuals are only to be valued for their increased contribution to social goals. But what are these goals? Economic prosperity is valuable only insofar as it is translated into the satisfaction of individual desires, the establishment of a secure peace valuable only because it allows individuals to pursue their activities without disruption, and so on. This illustrates once more my contention that, at bottom, socialistic dreams must be no less individualistic than the dreams of a perfect free market. It is only the corporate state, which either has aims of its own or which, like the Third Reich, is ordered according to the fantastic dreams of some dictator, that can deny the assertion that the individual is the ultimate touchstone of value. And such corporate states, I have argued, require us, implausibly, to deny the basic equality of all human beings.

But if the life of the individual *is* the ultimate touchstone of value, it is obvious that the individual must *have* a life, or rather, that there must *be* individual lives. This means that individual human beings have to be treated as originating centers of opinion, will, and desire, and for this to be true there must be some matters on which the word of the individual is final. Chief and most obvious of these are wants and desires. If we are to make sense of many of the things we value, we must make individual human beings ultimate bearers of that value (though not the only bearers), and this means acknowledging them as authorities on, among other things, what they want and what they believe. Their word on these matters must at some point be final just as we regard our own word on these things as final. "Don't tell me what I want" is a familiar way of asserting one's independent personhood, of drawing the line between what others may legitimately and what they may not legitimately do for us. The belief that there is such a line is what I am calling a belief in the separateness of persons.

Once more this line of thought raises deep and difficult questions, this time in philosophy rather than theology. At various points in their history Eastern and Western philosophy have brought into question the metaphysical belief that persons are separately identifiable unchanging entities. This convergence of opinion and the most forceful philosophical objections to the idea of personal identity are at the center of Derek Parfit's book *Reasons and Persons.*[9] Parfit argues that if we take certain facts about human biology seriously we must entertain the possibility of a single human organism being, over time, two or more persons, and of two or more human organisms being, over time, the same person, and since, furthermore there are no good philosophical arguments in favor of Cartesian egos, that is immaterial "souls" or centers of consciousness, we are obliged to conclude that distinct persons, as common belief thinks of these, simply do not exist. They are, rather, a false ideal to which we are attached. In this belief, he finds himself at one with the Buddha and, like the Buddha, welcomes the conclusion of his arguments as liberating.

Now someone impressed by these arguments might bring them to bear on my assertion of the separateness of persons in the following way. We can only believe that the separateness of persons ought to be respected if we believe that persons *are* separate. But Parfit's arguments show that what passes for discrete personal identity is only a matter of degree of psychological connectedness. In the deepest sense there *is* nothing to be respected here, for it is logically possible for a large group of individual human organisms to have a combination of psychological states such that we have no alternative but to describe them as one person. Just as a nation has no identity over and above the citizens who comprise it, so, Parfit wants to say, a person has no identity over and above the psychological states, i.e., memories, beliefs, hopes, and desires and so on, of which he or she is composed. And though Parfit himself does not develop the argument in this direction, it seems a small step to reason that we could actually seek the unification of different human organisms in one person. It follows that, in a deep metaphysical sense, a nation, a race, perhaps even the whole of humankind could be a single person. All this would need is a very high degree of psychological connectedness between all human beings, something to be accomplished, perhaps, through the ancient practices of Eastern mysticism. In this way, one might say, the idea of a world soul makes its appearance in Western philosophy.

Such a possibility appears to have a devastating effect on my own arguments. If a large *group* of human beings can form one person in just the same sense that *one* human being can be a person then respect for persons does not imply either an individualistic morality or an individualistic society as these are normally conceived, and there is an alternative to the free association of individual human beings which is not the objectionable corporate state.

Some will find Parfit's arguments, and the implications I have drawn from them, highly fanciful. Whatever their cogency they are, to my mind, of the greatest interest and show convincingly that the Western tendency to dismiss the more exotic elements of Eastern religion is ill-founded. Nevertheless, in the plain man's rejection of them there is something correct. Whatever logical possibilities we may entertain there seems no practical alternative to the assumption of the separateness of persons. Nor indeed, does Parfit's argument claim anything to the contrary. The argument, through its imagined cases, shows only that it is logically possible that two distinct organisms should be one person. Nothing shows or could show it to be false that, at present and for the foreseeable future, individual human beings will be related to persons on a one-to-one basis. If this is correct, then the only *practical* alternative to individualism is corporatism. And in this way, just as in the last section, the deep philosophical issues can be sidestepped if our interest is in the ethical beliefs it is right to have.

Such sidestepping is necessary if we are to bring the ethical arguments to a conclusion without settling or at least attempting to settle the very large issues that Parfit raises. And it is also justified. Nonetheless, there is always the feeling that such a move is *too* convenient, and that questions are being avoided which do not thereby go away. Any unease of this sort, however, need only attach to a secular liberalism, for I propose to show briefly, if I can, that Christian theology is not only compatible with Parfit's metaphysics of mind, but actually requires something of the sort, and can nonetheless explain the importance of the separateness of persons.

The first element of the theology to be borne in mind is God's creative activity. If we are persons as well as human animals, then we owe our personhood to God no less than our animal nature—our psychology as well as our biology. Traditionally, of course, Christians have envisaged the soul along

Platonic lines, something immortal and immaterial, brought into existence a short time after conception and continuing to exist after death. There are many well-known difficulties with such a view—How could incorporeal souls be related to physical bodies? How is one *post mortem* soul to be distinguished from another? What possible evidence could there be for the claim that an incorporeal soul *leaves* a body? and so on. But if we take the view that persons are not incorporeal entities but collections of connected psychological states held in a certain unity by physiological facts and continuing to exist only so long as those physiological facts continue to obtain, then, though a mystery is not eliminated (for it is still a puzzle as to how mental and physical states are related), we can see that God's creativity with respect to persons is just one aspect of His creativity with respect to the physical universe. And there is another advantage to construing the matter in this way. The Christian hope is for atonement, communion with God, that is, a becoming one with God. Now it is not easy to make sense of this notion, and indeed it is often said that communion of this sort is irreducibly mystical, but it seems clear at least that, if we conceive of persons as essentially discrete and indestructible spiritual particles, then there cannot be communion. For communion to be possible, whatever exactly it may be, it seems plainly necessary that the human soul should be able to undergo some measure of disintegration and reintegration in God. Now if we take the view that persons are neither Cartesian souls nor uniquely related to a single human organism we can give some account of the dissolution and perpetuation of persons in God. Moreover, remembering again God's physical creativity, we can reason that persons are separate because of their physical nature and, this being an expression of God's will, are separate because and as long as God wills it. Thus, for the Christian, the separateness of persons can in this way be seen to be an expression of God's will.

This, of course, is just the merest outline of how Christian theology might not only accommodate but exploit a physicalist philosophy of mind with its radical Parfittian implications. My business here, however, is only with answering the challenge that such a philosophy of mind might present to the fundamental liberal contention that a belief in the importance of separate individuals must lie at the heart of many of our evaluations. And my contention is that secular liberal morality may reasonably rest content with the practical necessity of making such an assumption, while Christian theology, by accepting the physicalist conception, might actually go further in explaining the value of separate persons as expressions of God's will in creation.

V

The basic equality of human beings and the importance of separateness of persons are fundamental features of liberal individualistic morality, and I have claimed that not only do we have good reason to accept these ideas in their own right, but that we can also find a basis for them in Christian theology as I have construed it in outline. The third feature of liberal morality mentioned earlier and remaining to be discussed is self-reliance. In many ways it is this one feature that marks off liberal morality of the libertarian sort, for while socialists of every stripe will not only accept but stress the basic equality of human beings (construed rather differently, of course, and with importantly different implications), and must, if I am right, accept the separateness of persons, they will not accept the value of self-reliance. They can allow, as anyone must, that social and historical circumstances may make self-reliance a characteristic that it is prudent or even essential to encourage; there are social conditions in which one is likely to be unable to call upon the help of others in practice. But the existence of such conditions gives us no reason to applaud them. We may still, consistently, work for a world in which we are reliant on others and they on us.

What marks off strict liberals is that they regard self-reliance as a virtue and something to be striven for even in a world in which the help of others *is* readily available. So, for instance, it is easy in the modern world to imagine societies in which a tolerably good standard of living is possible for those who are entirely dependent upon welfare programs, and even societies (the sort the free marketeer dreads) in which it is possible to have a *better* standard of living on welfare than if one works for oneself. Now the possibility of such societies shows that the basis of the liberal belief cannot be prudence. Just as the socialist must admit that times and circumstances can make self-reliance a necessity, so the liberal must admit that there are societies in which it simply is *not* imprudent to allow oneself to be wholly dependent upon the efforts and charity of others. Life for the recipient of welfare in many modern states is a great deal less precarious than life for the self-employed. The objection to "scroungers," then, must be to the character rather than the foolishness of their chosen position. What could this be?

One line of thought is this: no one can take a pride in his achievements who achieves nothing, and without some measure of pride there can be no self-respect. If respect for others in virtue of their humanity is a duty, so self-respect in virtue of one's own humanity is a duty. It follows that we have a duty to make a life for ourselves in which we can take a pride. This line of thought is not implausible, but I do not think it uncovers the real objection. Perpetual recipients of welfare benefit, leaving aside all the other things they might do with their time, can simply deny that they have accomplished nothing. Their achievement is to live tolerably well without arduous labor. Their accomplishment is a leisured life at a relatively low personal cost. They have, as they might say, "worked the system," and this is no less of an accomplishment than working in a factory and may, in terms of the intelligence and persistence it requires, be more so. Since a rejoinder of this kind obviously has some truth in it, any objection that is to be brought against this mode of life cannot rest upon the contention that "scroungers" have achieved nothing, but rather that what they have achieved is not a worthy accomplishment.

Why not? If we simply consider the characteristics required to live in the way they do and the sort of life that they lead as a result, we have no reason, I think, to regard it in any less favorable light than the lives of many of those who have jobs. There are jobs (like those in government bureaucracies as they are popularly imagined) which are wholly parasitic on the productive efforts of others and which contribute nothing of value to individual or social enterprises. They are merely ways of making a living. I do not mean to criticize the occupants of such posts or even to criticize the social arrangements which make these possible—only to point out that the employed can be as socially parasitic as the unemployed. It might be said, however, that the important difference lies in the intentions of the agent. The occupant of an office, however parasitic, means to work for a living whereas the "scrounger" does not. He means to exploit the social provisions under which those who genuinely cannot find employment—cannot, that is to say, prosper in self-reliance—are protected from the worst consequences of such misfortune. It is his attitude rather than his behavior that is at fault.

Now to my mind this is quite the wrong way to regard public welfare systems. The "exploitation" of these systems is not at all like the exploitation of someone's generosity. Those who are entitled to benefit have a legal right to it under the rule of law and should no more be thought to be in receipt of charity than the homebuyer who receives tax relief on his mortgage is to be regarded as in receipt of charity. The persistent recipient of welfare, who does not seek *more* than the rules entitle him to but is determined to get *all* that the rules entitle him to, is no different to the wealthy self-made man who does his utmost to avoid tax, though not to evade it. If the possibility of living a life of Riley on welfare benefit creates social or economic problems, then there is reason to change the rules, but the recipient of welfare has no greater obligation to avoid or prevent such problems than any other citizen.

There is an attitude, however, which may accompany the actions of the welfare recipient (though it may accompany the actions of the employee also) which *is* objectionable. This is not the attitude that seeks all and only that which the law allows but one which expresses the belief that the world owes us a living. What is wrong with such a view is that it allows selfish desire to distort reality—it is a form of false consciousness. People who believe that the world owes them a living cannot, or do not, take a detached and realistic view of their relations to others. Since it is possible to squander one's talents and resources, to alienate others, to exploit their kindness, and to destroy all claims of merit and desert, it must thereby be possible to be without a claim upon the world or an attachment to it. The assertion that the world owes me a living is the assertion, in effect, that I cannot sink so low, and since I *can*, it is for this reason that it is to be called a false consciousness. It is the counterpart, with respect to human beings, of the attitude which believes that God has *a duty* to save worthless sinners, an attitude which reveals an inability to acknowledge the necessity of God's *grace*.

Let us agree that such an attitude is objectionable. For present purposes we need to show that the belief that this is so is connected with a belief in the value of self-reliance. But I shall argue, to the contrary, that the proper basis of our objection to this attitude actually implies a rejection of the value of self-reliance and that this rejection is also implied by Christian theology. I shall then argue that it is in this way that charity can be seen to be a true Christian virtue.

The men and women who believe that the world owes them a living fail, in the circumstances I described, to acknowledge that in reality they have, by their own conduct, severed those relations upon which such an obligation might be founded. This does not alter the fact, however, that they still need the means whereby to live. They are not deserving poor, but they are poor, and true charity, which is concerned with need and not with desert, will not hesitate to supply their need. To say that the attitude is objectionable is to provide us with a reason to avoid coming to that condition, not a reason for ignoring those who are in it. Now it might be supposed that self-reliance is a virtue just because it is the opposite of this objectionable attitude. But this is not so. First we can be false-consciously self-reliant, and second we can acknowledge our dependence, even our total dependence upon others with a true consciousness.

By false consciousness I mean not simply mistaken beliefs (which are unavoidable in finite minds) but the set of beliefs resulting from an attitude of mind which leads us to prejudge most of the questions (or most of a certain range of questions) presented to us. In short, false consciousness is the understanding which results from a closed mind, true consciousness that which results from an open one. I use the term for much the same reason that Engels coined it, to draw attention to a mentality, different from merely parochial narrow-mindedness (which Burke and others have thought essential for a stable society), which engages or appears to engage in critical reflection, in considering the facts and the opinions of others, but whose conclusions are predictable and whose "thinking" is essentially idle. That there is such a mentality can hardly be doubted, though the Marxist thesis—that all historical, moral, political, and legal thinking is of this sort—can be shown to be false, I think.[10]

No one whose aim is knowledge, especially self-knowledge can want a false consciousness. This is not to say that no one can want one, or even that no one can rationally want one. A closed mind may enjoy a peace of mind that someone who knows how things really stand may not be able to enjoy, and since it is not always more rational to prefer knowledge to happiness, there can be contexts and occasions when it is rational to insulate oneself from the truth. This could not be rational for a Christian, however. The belief that eternal felicity, in this life and the next, lies only with God, and that self-knowledge is essential in the penitent and penitence essential if we are to stand right with God, makes knowledge a prerequisite of happiness. To show, therefore, that a self-reliant false consciousness is possible is to show, for the Christian, that self-reliance cannot in itself be a virtue. But it is not to show this to the satisfaction of the secular liberal. In the face of examples of false-conscious self-reliance liberals can assert that a sense of self-reliance is more important than knowledge and such a consciousness is thus to be preferred.

But are there such cases anyway? That there are seems to me something which it is easy to show. Everyone is familiar with occasions upon which adults permit children to harbor the false belief that they themselves have brought about something difficult when in fact it is the adult that has done so. There are plenty of good reasons for deceiving children in this way, but my point is that the child does not see, or is prevented from seeing, the whole context in which his action takes place and his true contribution to the outcome. Now while we may think it wrong to treat adults in this way, to give them an inflated idea of their own importance and abilities, this does not show that nothing of this sort ever happens. Furthermore, it says nothing, factual or moral, about those cases in which the belief is brought about by the agents themselves. It is, I am inclined to say, extremely easy for human beings to take an egocentric view of events in their lives and to overestimate the beneficial effects of their 'timely' words and 'prompt' actions. If so, it does not take much imagination to see that these overestimates may figure in their understanding of the contribution they have made to their own prosperity and status. In such cases, consequently, they mistake the degree of their self-reliance and may easily develop the mentality in which they habitually do this, a mentality superbly captured by Jane Austen in the character of Mrs. Norris in *Mansfield Park*.

Admittedly, this in itself does not show that self-reliance is no virtue, only that we can, habitually, be mistaken about our possession of that virtue. But false consciousness enters into self-reliance more deeply. To strive to rely upon oneself rather than others is to rely upon one's own opinion and judgment in preference to others, to prefer one's own efforts, however successful, to those of other people. This could only be reasonable if and insofar as one's own judgment *is* more reliable and one's own efforts more likely to be successful. In some cases, of course, this will be true, but for any human being it will

not be true in every case. Self-reliance, however, bids us prefer
our own efforts to those of others in every case and there can
be no good reason to do this. If the judgment of others or their
efforts in some respect are more likely to be satisfactory for us
than are our own, reason bids us prefer them, for I take it to
be an axiom of practical reason that one ought to prefer the
better to the worse. Where, on the other hand, our own judgments and efforts are more likely to be satisfactory we should
rely upon them, not because they are our own, but because
they are better. It follows that there is no virtue in *self*-reliance
as such.

I can imagine two plausible objections to this analysis. The
first is that it misdescribes the virtue in question and the second that it ignores the truth that there is value in doing something for oneself. The force of the first point is this: self-reliance
need not bid us foolishly to prefer our own efforts to those
of others regardless of their respective merits, but only to prefer to do ourselves those things which we can do *as well as*
others, and to develop in ourselves as many abilities as our
natural aptitudes will allow so that we may maximize the occasions upon which we are self-reliant with good reason.

But such an objection does not really undermine my analysis. To the extent that our own efforts are as good as others
we have reason to rely upon them, but no more reason to rely
upon them in preference to others, unless self-reliance is indeed something valuable, and we have no reason to maximize
these occasions unless the same holds true. This shows that
the first objection *presupposes* that self-reliance is a virtue; it
does not establish it as one. This leads to the second objection.

Self-reliance would be a virtue if we *did* have reason for this
preference. Such a reason might be said to lie in the fact that
there is value in doing things for oneself. To this I reply: there
is reason to do *some* things for oneself, precisely because the
involvement of self makes them what they are. But this is not
true for everything. So, for instance, I may prefer to play the
piano myself, badly, sometimes, rather than listen to the same
piece of music played much better by someone else. But this

is because 'piano playing' is something I want as well as 'listening to music'. If what I want is listening to music, and I can play as well as another, I cannot see that I *do* have reason to play myself. Which of us plays ought surely to be a matter of convenience or indifference.

If all this is true a striving for reliance upon self will inculcate a false consciousness just because it will prejudge the respective merits of our own efforts as against others. If self-reliance *were* a virtue, of course, we could allow that there must be some trade-off between the need to be self-reliant and the desirability of knowing the truth. But nothing we have encountered does give us reason to think this. The liberal individualist might, for reasons not as yet provided, incline to the belief that a *sense* of self-reliance is a something worth possessing even at the expense of self-knowledge. In this he would be like the utilitarian, who will think ignorance a price worth paying for happiness where the two conflict. But in so reasoning the liberal individualist would, as I implied earlier, only be calling upon a sense or *feeling* of self-reliance, not upon self-reliance itself.

I conclude, then, that positively to seek self-reliance for its own sake is to live false-consciously. It remains to establish the second of the two propositions asserted above—that we can acknowledge our dependence, even our total dependence upon others with a true consciousness.

It will be recalled that the attitude of those who believe the world owes them a living was found to be objectionable, chiefly because, in the clearest cases, the belief has brought it about that the world owes them nothing of the sort. For such people to survive at all they must depend upon the *grace* of others, which is precisely what, by their attitude, they deny. But there is another attitude, described by Kant in his discussion of the duty of charity in the *Groundwork to the Metaphysic of Morals*, which might be thought not to be objectionable in this way (and which may also be thought to be an expression of the attitude of self-reliance). This is the man who, while he refuses charity to others, asks no charity in return, and acknowledges that, should he be unable to provide for himself, his attitude commits him to suffer, even to perish, without complaint. Kant claims that such a view is consistent, but doubts that anyone apprised of the changes and chances of this fleeting world could actually will such to be the attitude of all humankind. This is a major concession in his argument since it admits into it an element which, by his own account, pure practical reason, i.e., practical reasoning of the most compelling sort, ought not to include, namely matters of empirical fact. But whether Kant introduces such elements consistently or not, we may allow that the attitude he describes, one in which the individual seeks all and only his rights and acknowledges all and only the rights of others, does fly in the face of important facts. For it is the case that anyone who did not permit himself to receive anything that was not his due, and gave nothing he did not owe, could hardly be said to have a human life at all. In particular, relations of affection could not be carried on on these terms. No one could *owe* it to me to love me, and no one could *repay* my love, even though they might reciprocate it. No one is *due* a birthday present or a friendly inquiry, and to try to conduct relations with family or friends along these lines is to introduce a mentality which has its proper home in politics and the market place. It is doubtful, in fact, whether even these can be conducted satisfactorily on a purely contractual, legalistic basis.[11]

This is not to assert the supremacy of personal relations over business relations, only to assert that both have their place, and that a life composed entirely of what Hegel calls "morality" would not be a human life as we know it. Now to acknowledge that life, willy-nilly, contains relationships in which we are the recipients of benefits which come to us through the free grace of others does not in itself imply any one attitude. One can imagine the man in Kant's example, acknowledging the fact as inevitable, but regretting it deeply and seeking to minimize the number of such relations in which he stands. Alternatively, one can imagine another who realizes the extent to which he is dependent on the free grace of others com-

ing to regard himself, for just that reason, as quite without resource and adopting an attitude of servile gratitude to all those
whose grace he receives. Both attitudes are, it seems to me,
neurotic. The first is like the attitude of someone who acknowledges reluctantly that, try as he might, his hands will get dirty,
and reacts, not by accommodating this fact to his endeavors,
but by giving up the endeavors themselves. The second, on
the other hand, is the one-sided attitude of the someone who,
though he recognizes his own indebtedness to others, cannot
recognize the indebtedness of others to him, is forever thank-
ing them, while failing to see that they have no right even to
his thanks.

The only sane attitude would itself be an expression of
grace — an acknowledgment of the good charity of others without either resentment or obsequiousness. Such an attitude is
often exemplified by invalids who are totally dependent upon
the ministrations of others and who slide into neither the bit-
terness of resentment nor the indignity of constant and ful-
some gratitude. In such cases, I contend, to hope or strive for
self-reliance is fantasy and to accept charity with grace the dig-
nified response of a true consciousness.

The cases I have been discussing involve relations between
human beings. If Christian theology is true, the extreme case
of the total invalid mirrors, in human terms, our relationship
to God. Every blessing, on this view, comes from God, and
it is simple ignorance to suppose that we can secure these things
except by His grace and favor. Christian theology does not imply fatalism, however. Those things which we can do for ourselves, by the grace of God, we ought to do for ourselves, for
it is no less presumptuous to think that they will be done for
us than to think that God has a duty to make our efforts prosper. The "God will provide" school of thought too often conceives of God as a sort of super–cosmos manager, the excellence of whose system relieves us of the necessity of taking
thought for the morrow.

In the light of this conception, and bearing in mind the
analogous position of the invalid, we may assert that the proper

response of the believer should itself be an expression of grace, neither the Promethean attitude of one who, recognizing his dependence, rages against the heavens nor the attitude of self-abasement, sometimes confused with penitence, which comes to regard human beings as worthless filth. The first rests upon the mistaken idea that He who creates has a duty to make his creation independent, and the second upon the blasphemous supposition that a benevolent and omnipotent God can create worthless filth. The first attitude, it seems to me, is the sin from which the New Testament bids us turn, and the second the sin into which excessive religiosity plunges us. The ethic of re- ⌐ pentance, that is the sort of conduct consistent with this understanding, will be the proper life of the Christian. And the objective of this book will be accomplished when we have located charity in that ethic. It is to this that we can now turn.

VI

A short summary of the argument up to this point may be useful. I claimed in chapter one that we cannot plausibly seek to construct a recognizably Christian ethic independently of the theological concerns of the New Testament. Central to these is the Kerygma of Acts, the proclamation of the coming Kingdom of God, prefigured in the life, death, and resurrection of Jesus of Nazareth. If we are to show, therefore, that charity is a Christian virtue we must locate its place in the ethics of repentance. Two conceptions of charity which have met with an enthusiastic welcome among some Christian writers, however, can be shown both to be inadequate in this respect and to be independently objectionable. The attempt to identify the exercise of charity, through pastoral counseling, with psychological healing and the conversion of charitable concerns into those of political and social justice despite their popularity are, I have argued, demonstrably inadequate. In arriving at these conclusions I have relied upon the contentions that people ought to be treated autonomously and that equal respect for the needs of others is an axiom without which we cannot make sense of our concern for the poor. In this fourth chapter I have been exploring the notions of individuality, equality, need, and right which underlie these contentions in an attempt to delineate more clearly the place of charity in the Christian scheme of things. What we have seen, I think, is that we must construe charitableness as an expression of the repentant's gracious response to God's grace.

At no point have I attempted to define charity. This is chiefly because I do not think definitions ever accomplish much. As Stephen Toulmin has said

> Definitions are like belts. The shorter they are, the more elastic they need to be. A short belt reveals nothing about its wearer: by stretching it can be made to fit almost anybody.[12]

The point is, there are uses and examples to which any definition must answer, and these are almost never sufficiently uniform to admit of simple definition. The desire for definitions dies hard, however, and perhaps this is because people still hope that the human sciences can proceed in the same manner as some mathematical sciences, which do have a place for definitions and axioms, and may thereby attain something of the same precision and certainty. But nothing of the sort is possible. Theology, philosophy, ethics must all rest content with conceptions of their subjects which will not always square with the uses of the words that name them, and the uncertainty of whose boundaries will inevitably leave some of their precise implications unclear. This is not incapacitating in any way, to my mind. Clarity of thought and cogency of reasoning will still be possible as long as we are careful about how words are being used in each of the contexts in which we reason. We can *make* clear our use of a term without thereby supposing ourselves to have given a definition which will serve on every, or even any, other occasion.

By 'charity', then, I shall mean an active concern to help others in their poverty and weakness. As the term is frequently used, and as I shall use it, this includes not merely alms-giving,

or even the giving of emotional support, but sympathetic understanding as well. Thinking the worst of others betrays a
meanness of spirit which is to be contrasted with charitableness, that is, the practice of giving and accepting the most
favorable reading of the actions and motives of others consistent with the facts. Commensurate with this is the attitude
which refuses to take pleasure in the wrongs of others and the
hardships that befall them, no matter how deserving. In this,
as in the respects discussed in chapter three, charity is at odds
with a lively sense of justice. In short, by charity I shall mean
pretty well what St. Paul describes as love in the thirteenth
chapter of first Corinthians. The question is: How exactly is
this related to penitence?

We saw that there can be at least three attitudes to the human condition – the attitude of self-reliance with its insistence
on rights, the attitude of self-abasement and obsequiousness
to others, and the gracious acknowledgment of our dependence.
These are, of course, extremes exemplified very rarely in the
attitudes of existing human beings, who commonly fluctuate
between these, and between other attitudes which it has not
been my business to describe. My contention is that the third
is the attitude which most properly respects the human condition as it actually is, and that if Christian theology is true,
and with it our total dependence on God, then it is the *only*
attitude which it is reasonable to try to adopt.

This is likely to be disputed, for, it will be said, whereas there
is a basic equality between human beings which makes the first
two attitudes inappropriate, there is a fundamental inequality
between humans and God. The third attitude is possible only
if we assume that God needs us as much as we need Him. But,
though some theologians have suggested that God does need
us as an object of love, this is, as Geach remarks,[13] to ignore
the doctrine of the Blessed Trinity, the very point of which
is to try and capture the truth that within one Godhead there
is the possibility of personal relations. Now if God does not
need us, and if He is as Christian theology portrays Him, there
is between God and us a gulf so great that nothing which re-

quires or even suggests an equal relationship can be correct. So, it might be said, the proper attitude *is* one of self-abasement, the sort of attitude expressed in this poem by Phineas Fletcher:

> My Lord? canst thou misspend,
> One word, misplace one look on me?
> Callst me thy love, thy friend?
> Can this poor soul the object be
> Of these love-glances, those life kindling eyes?
> See, I am black as night,
> See I am darkness: dark as hell.
> Lord, thou more fair than light;
> Heaven's sun thy shadow: can suns dwell
> With shades? twixt light and darkness what commerce?*

It is interesting that the necessity of such an attitude of mind might be brought in criticism against my argument by both the defender of orthodoxy *and* the critic of religion. The first calls attention to the fact that the proper attitude to God is one of worship, whereas it is always a mistake of the deepest sort to worship a human being. The second draws attention to the close similarity, perhaps identity, between the attitude of the truly humble and penitent worshipper, which is ineliminable from religion, and a pathological loathing of self. (Which does Fletcher express, for instance?) In their different ways both observations imply that my *via media* is not a properly religious attitude.

Now it must be conceded that the relationship between hu-

---

*It is interesting to compare Fletcher's poem with another, using similar images, by Thomas Campion

> View my Lord, a work of thine,
> Shall I then lie drowned in night
> Might Thy grace in me but shine
> I should seem made all of light.

Here, though human nature is thought of as night, its relationship to the light of grace is described in a way that transforms and does not merely stand in contrast to it.

mans and God cannot be wholly analogous to that between
two humans on any level or dimension. It is, of course, in keep-
ing with the method of Jesus in the New Testament, to construe the relationship of God to His creation in human terms
for the purpose of illuminating that relationship and helping
his hearers to understand it. So God is thought of, variously,
as shepherd, housewife, landowner, employer, plutocrat, and
above all as father. But all these analogies are limited and ought
not to be drawn out beyond that point at which they illuminate
the relationship. The difficulty, of course, is just to tell when
this point has been reached. One such analogy which I employed is that between the wholly dependent invalid and her
nurses, in which I claimed, we can see an acknowledgment of
total dependence without self-abasement. There remains in it,
one might say, an element of equality precisely because the fact
that it is *this* individual who is so dependent does not prevent
us from seeing that those who minister to her *could* themselves
have been in the same position. No such thought is applicable
to God.

But is this right? The most central of Christian doctrines
is that of the Incarnation. God need not become flesh, need
not be subject to human pain and frailty, but according to orthodox Christianity, this is precisely what He has chosen to
do. And He has done so in order that we might become one,
literally *commune* with Him. God's grace, in the Incarnation,
has made possible the seemingly impossible—the unity of man
and God. This is to be distinguished from their equality, of
course, but it remains the case that in such communion *two*
parties become one.

All this is paradoxical—which is to say that it invokes contradiction sooner or later, and usually sooner. There might be
either of two reasons for this—at the heart of religion lies the
necessarily mysterious and the doctrine of the Incarnation captures the essentially mysterious in one form, or at the heart
of religion is contradictory nonsense. It is not my purpose here
to settle this question. For my own part I think that anything
properly called religion will have to include some reference to

~(STA)

the essentially mysterious and will thus involve contradiction. Whether or not this is reason to abandon all religious belief is a separate question, but if it is true, we will have to tolerate some unresolved contradictions in theology, trying as best we can not to rest content with any that could be dispelled. One such contradiction, or paradox if you prefer, arises from the line of thought I have been following. Christians cannot speak of themselves as equal to God, though it is their gospel that God has chosen to make Himself equal to human beings, in order that a relation of atonement may be established (or re-established). In order to make sense of this at all we have to allow that individuals in becoming one with God do not, as one might suppose, lose their identity, but rather find their true identity. As the New Testament says, in a well-known passage:

> If any man would come after me, let him deny himself, take up his cross and follow me. For whoever would save his life will lose it, and whoever loses his life for my sake will find it. (Matt. 16:24)

There is no getting round the fact that this, as it stands, is flatly contradictory. We may for this reason dismiss it, or as I have been suggesting, for this very same reason, suppose that we have at last reached the heart of the matter. For my purposes I want just to assume that something like this will have to be said, if *anything* is to be said, and leave aside the question whether this is a mystery or mumbo-jumbo.[14]

Now if we do work on the assumption that there is a profound truth here, we will be able to see that the mode of life of the penitent will be one whose object is not merely "getting right with God," but getting right in the sorts of ways in which we may be said to be at one with Him. Plainly, there are respects in which this could *not* be done. We could not reasonably expect to be of one mind with God, since His knowledge is infinite and ours necessarily finite. Some suppose that we can become possessed of His *power*, that, for example through faith, we can heal as God heals and not as human beings customarily do. This form of communion, however, is contentious. But it is not contentious to suppose that our *will* can be one with His, that we can will those very things that He wills, not just in the sense that two individuals may will the same thing, but in the deeper sense in which St. Paul speaks of Christ working in him. That is to say, we can in our actions be the agents of a will "not ourselves, that works for righteousness," without its ceasing to be the case that the actions are ours (which is the mystery). And in acting and thinking charitably, I want to claim, this is precisely what we do.

The reason is that God's relationship to the world is one of continuous creation and the mode of that creation is love. The exercise of the charity St. Paul describes on the part of human beings is, therefore, a participation in that creative activity. To be concerned with the welfare of others as material, emotional, intellectual, and spiritual beings, and to acknowledge the value of their reciprocal concern for us is to live in God and hence to live creatively. This *must* be true, if Christian theology is true, but it is possible to consider the matter the other way about. If the life lived in Christian charity *is* creative (something which in principle, though rarely in practice, is empirically determinable) and a life of blessedness, then we have reason to believe that it is a life lived in God. According to St. Paul, all those things we think important in religion and elsewhere are flat and lifeless without the invigoration of charity. Why should we not raise the relatively straightforward question—is this true? And if the answer is positive, does this not imply something about the theology from which the life of charity springs? In this way we have returned to the issue raised and postponed at the end of chapter one: if the truth of Christian theology implies the desirability of the Christian ethic, does the desirability of the Christian ethic not imply the truth of Christian theology?

VII

There are those who have asserted that virtue is its own reward. I do not know that there are many who seriously believe this. It is easy to say "*fiat justitia, ruat coelum*," until there is a serious chance of the heavens falling. Besides which, the dictum conflicts with a deep conviction that the world is badly out of joint if the wicked prosper and the honest have no comfort other than the satisfaction of having done right. Kant has an argument for the existence of God which rests upon the contention that we cannot be rationally virtuous unless we suppose that ultimately true virtue will be crowned with happiness.

> Happiness is the condition of a rational being in the world, in whose existence everything goes according to wish and will. It thus rests on harmony of nature with his entire end.[15]

But since "there is not the slightest ground in the moral law for a necessary connection between the morality and proportionate happiness of a being," we must postulate the existence of a God whose benevolence and power can bring about such a result. If we do not, we can have no reason to act morally.

This argument has not found a great deal of favor among philosophers. One line of criticism insists that those who act rightly not because it is right but for some other end, like happiness, have a corrupt conception of the moral life—ironically a very Kantian sort of criticism. But to my mind there is something unrealistically high-minded about this attitude. If it were the case that everywhere virtue were crowned with *un*happiness so that to do what "morality" required was certain to be disastrous and always known as such, then I cannot see that it could be rational for a human being to regard moral considerations as overriding.

In fact Kant's argument, the objection to it, and my counterobjection all employ a distinction between "doing well" and "faring well," for which some moral philosophies have no place. Those Aristotelian and Christian moralities which make prudence a virtue, for instance, cannot draw the contrast in the way that Kant's moral philosophy does. On these views the desire and attempt to *fare* well form part of *doing* well. The difference is brought out most clearly in the concept of "the good life." On these views the good life for a human being (whether or not we understand this teleologically as Aristotle

does) is a mode of existence which cannot but commend itself
to human beings and cannot therefore work wholly contrary
to their desires and pleasures. In the light of Kantian moralities, on the other hand, there can be no unified conception
of the good life, because we must distinguish between the sort
of life we would most enjoy living and the sort of life it would
be right to live. On the first conception to say that virtue is
its own reward is unnecessary since the virtuous life is in part
determined by its character as a rewarding life. On the second,
the belief that virtue is its own reward is a belief we are driven
to precisely because the structure of morality *on this account*
can allow for the moral life to be utterly miserable.[16]

For my part I think that Christian morality must side with
the Aristotelians. Some have thought that it is easiest to construe the law of God with the moral law as Kant conceives
it, but this suggestion meets with the overwhelming objection
that it cannot accommodate God's creative activity, only His
character as lawmaker and judge. If we take seriously the idea
that God *creates* good and evil, then we cannot divorce the
ideal of flourishing from our ideas of the proper mode of any
creature's existence.

Of course, the Christian cannot regard the matter with Aristotle's rather smug complacency. As I have been stressing,
whether in point of fact the life of an individual flourishes or
fades is a matter of grace. There can be no question of working
out God's designs in such a way as to secure prosperity. Worship is not magic. But not everything is subject to chance and
uncertainty. *God* is not subject to change and His life is one
of eternal felicity. To live in God, therefore, is to attain a condition "where there is neither pain nor grief but life eternal,"
and it is the message of salvation that such a life, again by God's
grace, is possible for human beings. And given humankind's
creaturely, animal nature, this is precisely why the question
springs to mind "What is man that Thou are mindful of him?"
Once more, however, this eternal life is not something we can
secure; it is available only because God freely offers it, and to
be won by those who freely accept it.

For such a scheme of things to be plausible, I think, two non-theological propositions have to be true. First, it must be the case that eternal life has some features which human beings *qua* human beings can value. Some of the things we take to naturally in this life must be mirrored in the life eternal, even if they are only a foretaste of the heavenly banquet. Otherwise we have no reason to regard it as a condition of salvation. The prospect of listening forever to heavenly choirs can hardly be good news to those who hate music. This is not to say that there is no spiritual progress in the course of which individuals *fit* themselves for the Beatific vision, only that the first steps in such a development must commend themselves naturally. Second, the Christian way of living this mortal life must be enriching, both in those things which form the initial appeal of the Gospel and in those things which the life of the spirit uncovers as it develops. If it were not there would be nothing special to commend it and nothing to make us think that it made life a journey, as the psalmist says, "out of the pit and out of the miry clay" (Ps. 40). In short, the good news of salvation is only good news if the salvation it offers us is *from* those things we desire to avoid independently of it, and *to* those things (or some of them) which we desire. The life of the Christian can commend itself just insofar as it satisfies some of the deep longings of the human heart.

To this it will doubtless be replied that I have construed the Christian ethic as a recipe for successful living, something which Protestant popular preachers often do, but which presents a picture of it that is unfitting and quite false. Christians do not, on the whole, fare better than anyone else, nor have we any reason to think that they will since Jesus expressly warned his followers that they would in all likelihood be called upon to sacrifice many of the goods of this world.

Now to interpret my contention in this way is not altogether to mistake it, but it is to assume that we have a clear idea of what is to count as success. I do contend that the Christian way of life must hold out the hope (because based on the promise) of the sort of life that human beings will find the most satisfying, but I deny that we should automatically suppose this to be one in which material prosperity and social success figure prominently. And second, since I agree that the Christian life must be thought of as a "quest," I allow that it must, from the Christian point of view, be impossible to give a full description of the good life in advance of Christian discipline. What I do claim is that initially such an ethic must commend itself by its goodness for us *as we are now*, and not as we may become under its influence, and that since the Gospel must appeal to "all sorts and conditions of men," we must avoid making the good life the sort of life which will appeal only to those with a taste for spiritual asceticism or cathedral choirs. Sydney Smith's conception of heaven (eating *paté de foie gras* to the sound of trumpets) may be theologically suspect, but it has a ring of realism too.

Just what the good life is I do not mean to say, for this is a subject that would take a book to itself. I mean only to make the structural point that if we had such an account we would then be able to ask whether or not the way of life Christianity prescribes does indeed foster and further it. We should only be able to give an answer to this question, however, if we could also furnish an account of the Christian way of life. Once more I do not intend to do this, save to say that it must contain some element of prayer and worship. "Religionless Christianity," I shall assert, is no more possible than a non-theological Christian ethic, and it is only confusion which has allowed some people to call Christians those who never darken the door of a church and despise religious observances.

But if the proper description of the Christian way of life does include religious observances, though not only these, it might be supposed, contrary to what I have been saying, that it cannot provide a basis for the acceptance of Christian theology. It is only possible, sincerely, to ask God for things, to thank God, or petition Him if we are already, in the main, convinced that He exists and is as the New Testament portrays Him. "Oh God (if there is one), save my soul (if I have one)" can hardly be the standard form of prayer. If this is correct, however, the idea of coming to accept Christian theology because of the desirability of the Christian way of life is confused, since adopting the Christian way of life already presupposes the acceptance of Christian theology.

Now it seems to me that this overstates the case. For many Westerners at the present time the distinction between believer and unbeliever is not as clear as this implies. Though there are convinced fundamentalists and avowed atheists, there is also the finer distinction between "doubters within" and "doubters without." "Lord I believe, help Thou mine unbelief" *is* a familiar form of prayer. If so, it is not clear that there cannot be sincere attempts to pray by those who are uncertain whether anyone is listening. The logical point behind the objection is a good one, however. If the Christian way of life cannot be described properly without reference to practices whose rationality requires the truth of Christian theology, we cannot properly speak of some property that it may have providing us with a reason to accept that theology. What we can say, though, is that the satisfactoriness of those parts of the Christian ethic which are not religious observances gives us reason to explore, in practice, those observances. And if this requires us to nurture or even inculcate in ourselves some of the theological beliefs, that is reason to do so. This is no species of proof, certainly. Nor is it a species of rational strategy that is universally applicable, for there are many to whom the religious life is closed. But where the theological questions taken by themselves have left us uncertain, even to a small degree, then, as Pascal and William James argued, the desirability of the ethic supplies an alternative *and rational* entry to religious belief.

It is in this way that living in charity with one's neighbors becomes so important, for it is one such part of the Christian ethic. If living charitably, that is, responding to others in grace and not by right, proves creative and enriching we have reason to go further. The crucial question is, of course: Is charitable living deeply satisfying?

Many have thought it is. Even Geach, whose emphasis is

so much on love of God rather than man, commends charity because

> nothing blinds the heart more than malice; and contrariwise a disposition to construe one's neighbour's words as meaning something true or reasonable pays off in increased mutual understanding.[17]

Many would go much further and say that charity fosters *all* relationships and causes people to grow and flourish in the common life. Such claims may strike us as true, false, or simply over general. For my own part, I do not know how one would set about refining or establishing them as empirical generalizations. But I do not know that they need to be. The whole thrust of Pascal and James's strategy, which I have employed, is to insist that in this sort of case, as least, what confronts us (to quote Marx) "is not a question of theory, but a *practical* question. In practice man must prove the truth, that is, actuality, this-sidedness of his thinking."[18] Consequently, the resting place of the argument ought not to be in empirical generalizations, or worse, in attempts to establish them, but in the necessity to "try it and see."[19]

The result of the arguments we have been considering would thus appear to be a highly individualistic, almost existentialist view of Christian belief, one which denies that Christianity can have any social dimension at all and makes central to Christian ethics the response and the conduct of the individual. Such a conclusion will be highly unpalatable to a good many Christian thinkers, especially at the present time, if, that is to say, it really is as fiercely individualistic as this suggests, a question which I propose to consider in a final section.

VIII

There is a contrast commonly employed between different understandings of Christian belief according to which some make Christianity a matter of "personal" faith and others give it a more "social" dimension. Among the former are pietist, charismatic, and mystical versions of Christianity, among the latter moral rearmament, Christian Socialism, Catholic nationalism, and liberation theology. Such a contrast, however, relies upon a clear distinction between 'the personal' and 'the social' and it may be doubted first whether those who most readily contrast personal and social gospels have any clear understanding of this distinction, and second whether there is any such distinction to be drawn. The suggestion that my account of Christian ethics is too individualistic will best be countered, I believe, by an examination of this contrast.

As the terms are generally used it is not easy always to distinguish between 'society', 'culture', 'nation', and 'country'. Most commonly perhaps, people speak of a society as an entity with some sort of boundary which can be distinguished from other entities of the same sort, but since we properly speak of British and French society, Arab and Red Indian society, as well as Western and Communist society, it is evident that this boundary, if such there be, cannot be understood to be political or legal in any straightforward sense. In other words, 'societies' are not to be identified with 'nation states' and, I shall argue, it is only a confusion of the two which lends plausibility to the distinction between 'personal' and 'social' religion.

One way of showing that there is a real difference between society and the state is just to observe that any society is a network of different institutions and organizations, of which the state is only one. By 'the state' I mean that complex of people and offices which has a monopoly on the legitimate exercise of coercive power; that institution which, through law or force of arms, may compel individuals and groups to conform their behavior to its dictates. Thus understood, there is one clear use for the word 'political', which restricts it to describing those things pertaining to the organization or activities of the state.

Now sometimes when the Christian Gospel is said to have a social dimension, society and the state are confused, so that what is meant is that the Gospel has *political* implications, which is to say that Christians properly have views on what sort of state there ought to be. This, however, is a subject already dealt with. Broadly, I think that the liberal state with its heavy emphasis on individual liberties and equality before the law is the state most compatible with Christian theology, that for which the Christian has reason to strive and to preserve until the Kingdom of God shall have been made complete. Of course, it is precisely this emphasis on the individual which is under consideration, but my point is that my account of Christian belief (like any other I think) does have a political dimension, even if this is not in an approved direction.

If it does not have a sufficiently "social" emphasis, then, this must be 'social' in some other sense. But what sense could there be? People often speak of "Society" having a responsibility to the weak, the handicapped, the unemployed, and so on. What does this mean? It means, I think, that a society in which these groups are left to fend for themselves is morally repugnant. So much we might all agree with. Given that society is not the same thing as the state, however, it does not follow that a society in which there is no *state* provision for these things is morally repugnant. Furthermore, if someone should argue, as I have done, that Christian belief is not a proper ground for thinking that provision for these needs should lie with the state (on the ground that this is no less a case of what has come to be known as "moralizing the law" than are other instances, like outlawing homosexuality, more generally recognized to be objectionable), this cannot be taken to imply that there should be no *social* provision. What is in dispute is not the desirability of provision, but the source from which it should come.

Suppose we compile a list of services (suggested by Matthew 25, perhaps) which we agree those moved by Christian charity would approve of—hospitals, marriage guidance counselors, prison visitors, overseas aid and development agencies, schools for the handicapped, hospices for the terminally ill, and so on. We can imagine a society in which all these things are provided by the state and financed out of taxation. But we can also imagine a society in which they are provided with equal

PAROCHIAL SCHOOLS

success by independent, part voluntary part commercial, organizations, many of them church-run, and funded out of private donations, insurance schemes, lotteries, charity shops, sponsored events, television appeals, and so on. Remembering once more than we must not confuse society with the state, there seems no reason to deny that the second of these two imaginary societies is one which makes provision for the needy. It simply does not make it through the state.

Now the liberal individualism which I espouse may oblige Christians as such to forswear campaigns for state provision of social services (though, of course, there might be other *non-religious* grounds upon which these could be supported), but it does not oblige them to deny the value of these same services provided in other ways. Their belief ought to be, if I am right, that the individual is the ultimate touchstone of value and that it is to the individual that the Gospel speaks, but this does not carry the mad implication that individuals can do everything better on their own. Quite the contrary, in fact, for I stressed the Christian rejection of self-reliance. They can readily agree that individuals must work together if there really are to be good works which glorify their Father in heaven, and that true Christian charity requires them to do all that they can to assist in them. It is in this sense that Christian individualism can embrace public charity and does not restrict itself to personal alms-giving of a modest sort. What it cannot give us grounds to support is the dominant idea of almost all political parties in the West at the present time—that the state is the natural and obvious instrument for remedying all and every ill that may beset humanity. But why should we accept this belief in any case?

One answer, common even among the heads of the largest voluntary organizations, is that charitable good works cannot by themselves effect real change, that only the state has sufficient means to remedy ills on the scale that is needed. The question of effectiveness is an empirically factual one, of course, and well beyond the scope of this book. I shall have to conclude, therefore, with an expression of skepticism about the efficacy of the state in these things, and a corresponding optimism about the potentiality of private and voluntary agencies. But in favor of both the skepticism and the optimism something may be said. State agencies tend to bureaucracy and corruption. This is a function of their power and size. Thus that very same feature in which the political programs of Christians and others put their trust is also the source of their weakness. Second, all good charities recognize the necessity of self-help. Self-help schemes, however, provide for a dissemination of power, and this is more likely to be hindered than promoted by the use of centralized state agencies. Third, modern mass communication has greatly increased the potential of private and voluntary organizations, whose efficiency, accordingly, it is easy for us to underestimate.

These brief considerations do little to establish the superiority of non-state agencies in effectiveness. My arguments have been concerned with what it is right for the Christian (and others) to aspire to, and it is on these that I must rely. Nevertheless, there is much to be said for the belief that the modern nation-state, which is so easily and often regarded as a universal provider, is not only a recent creation, but a transient one also, and one furthermore that we are better off without. If so, and if my arguments are correct, Christian theology *is* liberation theology, since it frees us from a mistaken faith and hope in the redemptive powers of the state.

The argument is now complete. What I have attempted to show is how charity, in attitudes as well as actions, is an integral part of the response of the truly penitent seeking to realize the Kingdom of God. A proper understanding of this great virtue, I believe, brings into question much that is fashionable in contemporary Christian ethics, and especially ideas which despite being endorsed at the very heart of establishment opinion still pass for radical. If my arguments cause these beliefs to be examined again, they will have met with all the success they merit.

APPENDIX:

CHRISTIANITY AND MARXISM

The twentieth century has witnessed an interesting fluc-
tuation in the perceived relations between Christianity
and Marxism. The two began the century sworn enemies, so
much so that Christian churches and movements were generally drawn to the support of right-wing parties in a cooperative
battle against the forces of darkness, and communists for their
part regarded the elimination of religion and the destruction
of the church as one of their principal aims.

After the war, though Americans by and large continued
to regard Marxists and communists as dangerous atheists, the
Christian and the communist parties of Western Europe recognized the need to find some *modus vivendi* since neither, it
seemed, was about to disappear. Moreover, behind the Iron Cur-
tain it became increasingly clear that "God was not yet dead"
and that Marxist theoreticians must take account of this fact.
(*God is not yet dead* was the title of a book by the Czech socialist philosopher Vitezslav Gardavsky, one of the leading figures in the Christian-Marxist dialogue in Czechoslovakia during the 1960s.)

To this general political background was added an increasing crisis of confidence on the part of European Christians.
Curiously, it was not in communist countries that popular attachment to religion started to decline dramatically, but in the

relatively prosperous capitalist countries. The flight from established religion led many Christian activists to seek ways in which the Gospel message might be made 'relevant'. One way was the 'modernization' of ancient ecclesiastical and liturgical practices. Another was the identification of Christianity with the causes of political radicalism. In the 1960s there were many who thought that Christianity would recover its appeal if it was seen as a force for deep, even revolutionary, social and political change.

It was not difficult to move from this belief to a closer alliance with Marxism. If both Christians and Marxists were for revolutionizing the world, so the story ran, they *must* have a lot in common. The rather obvious stumbling block to a close alliance, namely that Marxist theory sees no place for religion among the forces of change nor the final constitution of society, was overcome to a degree by the talk of 'demythologizing' the Christian religion. What Marx and Marxists meant to condemn, namely obscurantist God-talk, modern Christian understanding of the Bible also regarded as out of date and misleading. And so it came about that people could describe themselves as Christian and Marxist, though it is worth remarking that this *rapprochement* was always a little one sided; Christians became Marxists, but Marxists (even sympathetic ones like Gardavsky) rarely became Christians, or if they did they converted to varieties of Christianity which required abandoning their Marxism. Nevertheless, in this context there was rhetorical value in Christians calling themselves Marxists; it signaled that they were on the right side.

Twenty years later the position has changed again. Those who find in Christianity radical social and political implications are still inclined to look favorably upon Marxist movements and Marxist language. But they have also seen that out and out alliance with Marxism as a creed is indeed impossible for self-professed Christians. Their advertized approach is thus much more cautious and critical than was common among the enthusiasts of the 1960s. It is an approach very clearly expressed by two of the best known liberation theologians, Leonardo and Clodovis Boff.

> In liberation theology, Marxism is never treated as a subject on its own but always *from and in relation to the poor*. Placing themselves firmly on the side of the poor, liberation theologians ask Marx: "What can you tell us about the situation of poverty and ways of overcoming it?" Here Marxists are submitted to the judgment of the poor and their cause, and not the other way round.
>
> Therefore, liberation theology uses Marxism purely as an *instrument*. It does not venerate it as it venerates the gospel. And it feels no obligation to account to social scientists for any use it may make—correct or otherwise—of Marxist terminology and ideas, though it does feel obliged to account to the poor, to their faith and hope, and to the ecclesial community, for such use. To put it in more specific terms, liberation theology freely borrows from Marxism certain "methodological pointers" that have proved fruitful in understanding the world of the oppressed, such as:
>
> * the importance of economic factors;
> * attention to the class struggle;
> * the mystifying power of ideologies, including religious ones. . . .
>
> Liberation theology, therefore, maintains a decidedly critical stance to Marxism. Marx (like any other Marxist) can be a companion on the way, . . . but he can never be *the* guide, because "You have only one teacher, the Christ" (Matt. 23:10).
>
> *Introducing Liberation Theology* (Maryknoll, New York, 1987), p. 28 (original emphasis)

Such an appeal must seem to many unobjectionable, a sensible openmindedness to helpful sources wherever they are to be found. But upon examination, this approach to Marxism turns out to be not much less rhetorical or uncritical than its predecessor. References to Marxism remain the stock in trade of radical Christians because of their oratorical force, not because of their theoretical superiority. They are thought to show Chris-

tian theologians to be on the right side in the great battle between good and evil.

To see this, consider how difficult it is to imagine the Boffs
writing the same things about capitalist economics as they do
about Marxism. Yet there is no reason in principle why the
theories of the free market should not have something to tell
us about "the situation of poverty and ways of overcoming it,"
and some reason to think that in practice they will. When it
comes to wealth creation, whatever about distribution, enterprise economics appears to be much more successful than socialistic planning along the lines of Eastern Europe. An open-
minded liberation theology would be open to this too; *anything*
that can help the lot of the poor is welcome. Yet Marxism is
mentioned and the free market is not. The difference lies in
the rhetoric.

Nor is the Boffs' approach as critical as it declares itself to
be. We are told that Marx is asked what he has to say that
is useful to liberation theology. But why ask *Marx?* Is it at all
likely that a man whose thought and empirical inquiries are
rooted in mid-nineteenth-century Britain and Germany will
have anything at all to say relevant to the context of late
twentieth-century South America? One may as plausibly turn
to the writings of Nassau Senior or Alfred Marshal, two other
nineteenth-century economists. But of course no one does;
their names have none of the *frisson* of radicalism.

We are told that what liberation theology can derive from
Marxism are "methodological pointers." These include "the importance of economic factors." But what does this point us to?
As it stands, the pointer is open to all the criticism leveled at
the "methods" of the psychotherapists discussed in chapter two.
It is unhelpful to tell us that economic factors are important;
we need to know just how important, and in what ways, before our explanations are any more powerful or our understanding improved.

On this point Marx himself was quite clear, of course. Economic factors are *the* determinants of all social and political
change. He had a very general theory of history which pur-

ported to bear this out, and which pointed to the way the future would go. An important part of that theory declared religion to be an 'opiate'. This idea has often been misunderstood. Marx's view was that in circumstances where economic forces made life for ordinary people next to intolerable, religion served the useful function of a painkiller, as opiates do to those in physical pain. But just as when health is restored we no longer need painkillers, so once the new economic order is ushered in, there will be no need for religion. When people have the power and resources to secure their own future, to make their own history as Marx puts it, they will no longer have either the need or desire to call upon God or look to the life to come. In the world of which communism dreams, religion is redundant.

What this shows is that if we take the "methodological pointer" seriously, we must see the end of the road for religion. The belief that fundamentally it is economic factors that matter allows us to dispense with any explanatory appeal to God or the workings of the Spirit, and to look for a world in which human beings are no longer driven by necessity to make such worthless appeals. The true Marxist yearns for this world, which can only be described as one in which people have become wholly indifferent to religion. How then can there be an alliance with Christians designed to bring about this world?

The truth is that Christian association with Marxism is not critical enough. As I have argued in the preceding chapters, I wholeheartedly endorse the idea that Christians should do all in their power to address the claims of the needy, and make use of whatever is helpful to this end. But I also believe, and think I can demonstrate, that Marxist theory, though of historical interest, is now known to be hopelessly flawed and will not provide any enhanced understanding of poverty and its causes. From this point of view, it is certainly time to look elsewhere.

More importantly, from the rhetorical point of view it is time for a change also. As the colossus of Eastern Europe begins to disintegrate, the idea that Marxism has much to do with liberation must have a less and less convincing ring to more and more people. For my part, I do not think that any Christian gospel, however radical its aspirations, needs to be trucked out with Marxist language, or that it can effectively be so trucked out for much longer. God is not yet dead, but Marxism is.

NOTES

1. Kerygma and Ethics

1. On this division, see Birger Gerhardsson, *The Ethos of Christianity*, trans. Stephen Westerholm (London, 1982).

2. For evidence of this variety, see Robin Gill, *A Textbook of Christian Ethics* (Edinburgh, 1985). Even this comprehensive volume does not exhibit the full variety since there are no excerpts from Calvin.

3. See Matthew Arnold, *God and the Bible* (London, 1875); R. B. Braithwaite, "An Empiricist's View of the Nature of Religious Beliefs," Eddington Memorial lecture (Cambridge, 1955), reprinted in *Philosophy of Religion*, ed. Basil Mitchell (Oxford, 1971); Don Cupitt, *The World to Come* (London, 1982); Stewart Sutherland, *Jesus, God and History* (Oxford, 1983).

4. This is one of the central concerns of Sidgwick's *Methods of Ethics*. For a more recent treatment, see Thomas Nagel, *The Possibility of Altruism* (Oxford, 1972).

5. On this, see William Barclay, *The Letters of James and Peter*, rev. ed. (Edinburgh, 1976).

6. There are important questions of biblical criticism involved here. For an expansion of many of the claims made in this paragraph, see *Understanding the New Testament*, ed. O. Jessie Lace (Cambridge, 1965).

7. On this point, see G. E. M. Anscombe, "Modern Moral Philosophy" in *Collected Philosophical Papers*, vol. II (Oxford, 1981).

8. The claim is defended at length in D. M. Baillie, *God was in Christ* (London, 1948), a book to which I owe a great deal.

9. See C. H. Dodd, *The Parables of the Kingdom*, rev. ed. (London, 1961).

10. This is an immense subject and centers chiefly on the historical veracity of the Gospels and the proper interpretation of the life

of Jesus. The following books form a small selection of the different critical viewpoints from which the investigation may be conducted: E. F. Scott, *The Validity of the Gospel Record* (London, 1938); Günther Bornkamm, *Jesus of Nazareth* (London, 1961); Michael Grant, *Jesus: An Historian's Review of the Gospels* (New York, 1978); F. F. Bruce, *The Real Jesus* (London, 1985); Ian Wilson, *Jesus: The Evidence* (London, 1984); and C. Leslie Mitton, *Jesus: The Fact Behind the Faith* (Grand Rapids, 1974).

11. For an elaboration of some of the relevant points here, see S. R. L. Clark, "God, Good and Evil" in *Is It Reasonable to Believe in God?*, ed. J. Houston (Edinburgh, 1985).

12. Reflected in these and earlier comments on the Beatitudes is the great amount I have learned from *The Way of Blessedness*, a study of the Beatitudes by Stuart Blanch (London, 1987).

13. See, for instance, R. C. Zaehner, *Our Savage God* (London, 1974).

14. For an extended discussion of this and other points, see I. C. M. Fairweather and J. I. H. McDonald, *The Quest for Christian Ethics* (Edinburgh, 1984).

15. A comprehensive discussion of the problem of evil is to be found in John Hick, *Evil and the God of Love* (London, 1966).

16. A very human instance of the interplay between belief and despair is to be found in the wartime reminiscences of Donald Caskie, the Scots minister in Paris, in *The Tartan Pimpernel* (London, 1957).

2. Charity and Counseling

1. See for instance, Charles V. Gerkin, *The Living Human Document: Re-visioning Pastoral Counseling in a Hermeneutical Mode* (Nashville, 1984).

2. Most notable of those who have had a radical change of mind is Thomas C. Oden, *Care of Souls in the Classic Tradition* (Philadelphia, 1984).

3. Among the most influential writings of this sort are Seward Hiltner, *Pastoral Counseling* (Nashville, 1949); Howard Clinebell, *Basic Types of Pastoral Counseling* (Nashville, 1966); Wayne E. Oates, *Pastoral Counseling* (Philadelphia, 1974); Carrol A. Wise, *Pastoral Counseling* (New York, 1951).

4. A. C. R. Skynner, "Development of Conjoint Family Therapy," in *Family Therapy in Social Work,* ed. W. H. Finn (London, 1974), 8.

5. A. M. Hertoghe and G. McLaine, "Family Therapy within a Casework Agency," in *Family Therapy in Social Work,* 44.

6. C. G. Fitzgerald, STD, and William Hammelman, OSB, "The

Interface of Pediatric Oncology and the Family," *Journal of Pastoral Care* 36 (1982): 27–28.

7. Homer L. Hernigan, "Preface to a Research Project in Pastoral Counseling," *Journal of Pastoral Care* 35 (1981): 76.

8. John Palton, "Clinical Hermeneutics: Soft Focus in Pastoral Counseling and Theology," *Journal of Pastoral Care* 35 (1981): 157.

9. Among the most influential are Karl Menninger, with Martin Mayman and Paul Pruyser, *The Vital Balance: The Life Process in Mental Illness and Health* (New York, 1963); Carl R. Rogers, *On Becoming a Person* (Boston, 1961); Carrol A. Wise, *Pastoral Psychotherapy* (New York, 1980).

10. Even a brief survey of issues of the *Journal of Pastoral Care* will confirm this.

11. John Foskett, *Meaning in Madness* (London, 1984).

12. *Journal of Pastoral Care* 36 (1982): 74.

13. Charles W. Stewart, in a review of *Pastoral Psychotherapy: Theory and Practice* by Carroll A. Wise, *Journal of Pastoral Care* 35 (1981): 126.

14. This is now a widely shared view. For the latest (of many) discussions, see Adolf Grünbaum, *Foundations of Psychoanalysis* (Berkeley and Los Angeles, 1984) and H. J. Eysenck, *Decline and Fall of the Freudian Empire* (London, 1985).

15. *Small Group Psychotherapy*, ed. Henry Walton (Harmondsworth, 1971), 15.

16. C. R. Rogers, *Client Centered Therapy* (Boston, 1951), 20.

17. Ibid., 139.

18. *Casebook in Pastoral Counseling*, ed. N. S. Cryer, Jr., and J. M. Vayhinger (New York, 1962).

19. Ibid., p. 272.

20. *Small Group Psychotherapy*, 11.

21. Robert Nozick, *Philosophical Explanations* (Oxford, 1983).

22. For a discussion of these issues, see H. J. Paton, *The Categorical Imperative* (London, 1947).

23. For a lucid general discussion of these matters, see R. Downie and E. Telfer, *Respect for Persons* (London, 1969).

24. *Small Group Psychotherapy*, 62–63.

25. Ibid., 80.

26. Ibid., 47.

27. This is directly contrary to the opinion of one writer, Thomas C. Oden, who in his earlier work claimed to find in Rogers's expressly secular counseling a deeply Christian theology. But see note 2 above.

28. C. D. Kean, *Christian Faith and Pastoral Care* (London, 1961).

29. Ibid., 41.

30. Ibid., 80.

31. On this, see *Nuclear Weapons and Christian Conscience* (London, 1963) and *The Church and the Bomb* (London, 1983).

32. For some further reflections on this theme, see my "Commitment and the Value of Marriage," in *Person to Person*, ed. George Graham and Hugh LaFollette (Philadelphia, 1989).

33. This topic, together with the attractions of the Aristotelian conception, is the theme of Mary Midgley, *Beast and Man* (London, 1978), and Alasdair MacIntyre, *After Virtue* (London, 1981).

34. On this, see Fairweather and McDonald, *The Quest for Christian Ethics*, referred to in chapter one.

3. Charity and Political Action

1. Torres's politicization was completed when he left the priesthood and joined the National Liberation of Colombia, declaring "I believe that the revolutionary combat is a Christian and priestly combat. . . . It is the only way, in the concrete circumstances of our country, for us to love our neighbour as we should." See Dennis P. McCann, *Christian Realism and Liberation Theology* (New York, 1981), 143–44.

2. This view is forcefully expressed in the Kairos document, a theological comment on the political crisis in South Africa, issued by a large interdenominational group of South African theologians, and published in London in 1985.

3. Gustavo Gutierrez, *A Theology of Liberation*, trans. Inda and Eagleson (New York, 1973). The issue is comprehensively discussed in McCann, *Christian Realism and Liberation Theology*, chap. 7.

4. Well-intentioned sentiment, whose underlying assumptions remain crucially unexamined, marks the Kairos Document referred to above. Good intention is also more evident than analysis, evidence, and argument in Robert McAfee Brown, *Theology in a New Key* (Philadelphia, 1978). The style of 'argument' by bald assertion is to be found in Richard Norman's Reith Lectures *Christianity and World Order* (Oxford, 1978). Both Gutierrez and Miranda, it seems to me, allow their desire to be on the right side to overrule more hard-headed historical inquiry and biblical criticism. In this chapter I shall say a good deal in criticism of liberation theologians, but I should also record that their understanding of the Kingdom of God is very similar to the interpretation offered in chapter one.

5. This is a version of the arguments offered by St. Thomas Aquinas in his discussion of the relation between human and divine law (*Summa Theologica*, I–II, q. 90–108).

6. In *On Princely Government, Aquinas Selected Political Writings*, ed. A. P. D'Entreves (Oxford, 1959).

7. In *Martin Luther: Selections from His Writings*, ed. John Dillenberger (New York, 1961).

8. Juan Luis Segundo "Social Justice and Revolution," *America* (April 1968). A general view of Segundo's extensive writings will be found in Alfred T. Hennelly, *Theologies in Conflict* (1979).

9. Gutierrez, *A Theology of Liberation*.

10. In *The Gospel of Peace and Justice*, ed. Joseph Gremillion (New York, 1976), 447.

11. *Faith in the City (The Popular Version)* (London 1985), 6.

12. The list of books and other publications with this as their theme is almost endless. Representative are *Cry Justice* (London, 1984) by John de Gruchy, Professor of Christian Studies in the University of Capetown; *Bias to the Poor* (London, 1983) by David Sheppard, Anglican Bishop of Liverpool; *Faith and Freedom* (Belfast, 1979) by Schubert M. Ogden; and *Justice on the Agenda* (Basingstoke, 1985) by Roger Sainsbury.

13. Extracted in Gill, *A Textbook of Christian Ethics*, 278.

14. See note 4 above.

15. See John Rawls, *A Theory of Justice* (Boston and Oxford, 1972); Robert Nozick, *Anarchy, State, and Utopia* (Oxford, 1974); and Anthony Flew, *The Politics of Procrustes* (London 1981).

16. A philosophical view opposed to that elaborated here will be found in Henry Shue, *Basic Rights* (Princeton, 1980).

17. Oxfam pamphlet, "Hungry for Change," 1984.

18. For a discussion of some of these difficulties, see Julian L. Symon, "Resources, Overpopulation, Environment: An Oversupply of False Bad News," *Science* 208 (June 1980).

19. These issues are fully examined in P. T. Bauer, *Dissent on Development* (London, 1971).

20. Ted Honderich discusses this general point in an appropriate context in *Violence for Equality* (Harmondsworth, 1980).

21. On this see Bauer, *Dissent on Development*.

22. P. T. Bauer, *Equality, the Third World and Economic Delusion* (London, 1981), 75.

23. Quoted from a War on Want pamphlet in ibid., 76.

24. See Peter Laslett, "The Conversation Between the Generations" in *Philosophy, Politics and Society*, fifth series, ed. Laslett and Fishkin, (Oxford, 1980).

25. This inclination continues in the use of the expression 'People of God' in the writings of many liberation theologians. See McCann, *Christian Realism and Liberation Theology*, 213–217.

26. On this, see Christopher Dawson, "God's Creation, Wealth

Creation and the Idle Distributors" in *The Kindness that Kills*, ed. Digby Anderson (London, 1984).

27. A beautiful portrait of the underlying clash of values between East and West here is to be found in Rudyard Kipling's *Kim*.

4. Charity and Repentance

1. Peter Geach, *The Virtues* (Cambridge, 1977).

2. On this, see Gerhardsson, *The Ethos of Christianity*, chap. 4.

3. Peter Geach, *God and the Soul* (London, 1969).

4. On this point in relation to the problem of evil, see Alvin Plantinga "The Free Will Defense" in *Philosophy of Religion*, ed. Basil Mitchell (Oxford, 1971).

5. An overview of the arguments rehearsed here will be found in Steven Lukes, "Taking Morality Seriously" in *Morality and Objectivity*, ed. T. Honderich (London, 1985).

6. This assumption of superiority is found most clearly in No. 8 of the Fascist Decalogue which states "Mussolini is Always Right."

7. This possibility is well illustrated in David Yallop's *In God's Name*. Whether all he says about the Vatican is true I am not in a position to judge, but the fact that it *could* be true is enough to illustrate my point.

8. For instance, making it a crime to go about on Christmas Day "as though it were a holiday."

9. Derek Parfit, *Reasons and Persons* (Oxford, 1984).

10. A defense of this claim will be found in chapter three of my *Politics in Its Place* (Oxford, 1985).

11. Much modern thought has, nevertheless, moved in this direction. See David Gauthier, "The Social Contract as Ideology," *Philosophy and Public Affairs* 6 (1976–77).

12. Stephen Toulmin, *Foresight and Understanding* (London, 1961), 18.

13. Geach, *The Virtues*, 71–72.

14. For some further thoughts on this, see my "Mystery and Mumbo-jumbo," *Philosophical Investigations* 9 (1984).

15. Immanuel Kant, *Critique of Practical Reason*, trans. Lewis White Beck (Indianapolis, 1956), 129.

16. An amplification of these brief remarks will be found in my *The Good Life: An Introduction to Moral Philosophy* (New York, 1990).

17. Geach, *The Virtues*, 86.

18. Karl Marx, *Theses on Feuerbach*, XI.

19. Some of the lines of thought implied are interestingly explored by Frederick Sontag in "Three Ways," *Scottish Journal of Theology* 40 (1986).

INDEX